Sunset Ideas for
Landscaping

By the Editors of Sunset Books and Sunset Magazine

LANE BOOKS
MENLO PARK, CALIFORNIA

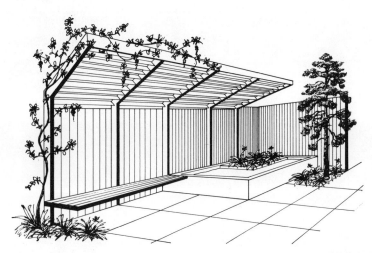

Edited by Elizabeth Hogan

Cover: Various landscaping elements are effectively combined
in this design: lawn, border plantings, steps, raised beds,
walkway. Mature trees shade and shadow terrace; petunias add
seasonal color. Mushroom lamp provides soft light for plants,
needed light for steps. Landscape architect: Thomas
Church. Photographed by Ells Marugg.
Cover design consultant: John Flack.

Illustrations: Gary J. Patterson

Second Printing May 1972

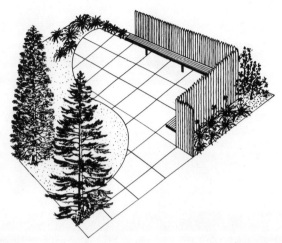

Contents

Border *of daffodils, perennials provide year-round show of color. Fig trees are espaliered along fence.*

Enclosed streetside patio *was designed for easy care. Abundance of color comes from containers of petunias. Bougainvillea on roof, cymbidiums, Hawaiian tree fern under overhang, banana at far right thrive here.*

An Introduction to Landscaping

A different concept of landscaping developed when homeowners decided they wanted to cook and entertain out-of-doors. Generally, they found that their garden or back yard was not designed for outdoor living. There was no privacy; tables and chairs poked holes in the lawn; often the sun was too hot, the wind too strong, the evenings too chilly.

Obviously, before outdoor space could be used, it had to be made more habitable. If much the same kind of living was to take place outdoors as indoors, the same problems had to be solved—furniture arrangement; pathways for circulation; a floor of some sort for tables and chairs; walls, fences, or hedges for privacy; and some sort of climate control. Factors seldom dealt with previously in conventional landscaping became important. Landscaping meant designing the garden not only for beauty, but also for comfort. It meant paving a patio, constructing a deck, devising a sun or wind screen, installing lights, or building a roof over a garden corner. Landscaping summed up all the things one did to make the garden more livable.

Cool, green, *ferny look of deep dark woods is due to sycamores and leaning oak native to site, leatherleaf ferns beneath trees, wild strawberry ground cover. Plants have year-round greenness, perform well in shade.*

Landscaping, wherever it occurs—New York, Atlanta, Chicago, Denver, Seattle, or Los Angeles—involves the same guiding principles of weather control and adaptability to people's needs and desires. You can choose to accept or reject gardening; to be absorbed in the arrangement of flowers, shrubs, and trees, or just sit in the shade; to enjoy close communion with plants, or to be involved with people; to create a garden picture from a kitchen window or to borrow space from a garden by extending the living room into it.

LANDSCAPE FOR PEOPLE

Landscaping's first concern should be for people—their activities and comfort in the garden. People, seeking ways to satisfy their varying interests out-of-doors, are the measuring stick of effective landscape design.

• Their height is the scale against which the sizes of fences, shrubs, trees, and all vertical and overhead elements should be measured.

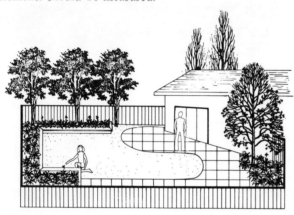

• Their line of vision determines whether a fence will provide privacy or merely separation.

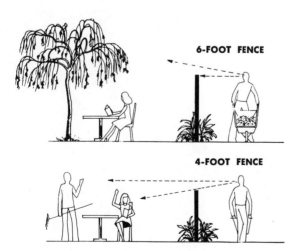

• Their purpose for planting a tree influences the kind of tree they will plant—shade trees to walk under; tall, dense trees for privacy; decorative trees to gaze upon.

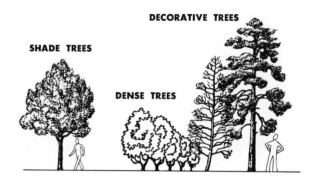

• Their height and line of vision size up garden spaces as being small and limited or large and expansive.

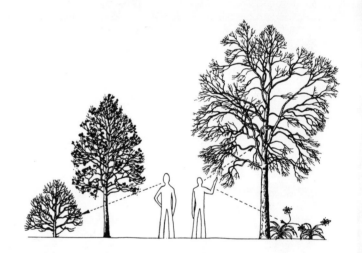

• Their reason for selecting a ground cover or shrubs decides the best height for a particular planting—ankle-high to cover the ground; knee-high for direction or traffic control; waist-high for partial enclosure; chest-high for division of space; above eye level for privacy.

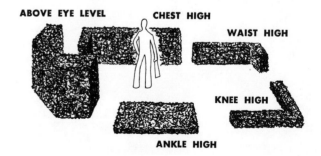

• People in motion outdoors require more space than they do when moving inside the house. Two people can walk side by side on a 4-foot garden path, but a 5-foot width gives them freedom to stroll and raise their eyes from the path.

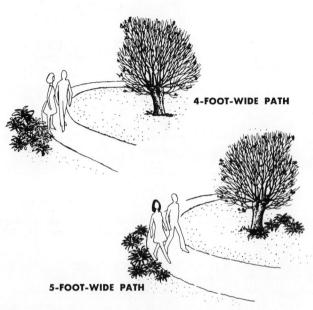

4-FOOT-WIDE PATH

5-FOOT-WIDE PATH

• Any equipment people might carry determines the width of gates, passageways, and other openings.

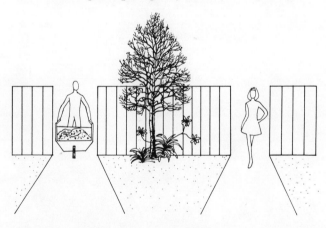

• Outdoors, people need storage space; the amount of room needed depends on the sizes and amount of tools and equipment.

• The space people need for relaxing or entertaining should determine the size of the patio. Their sitting position determines the height of a seat wall, benches, and other structures.

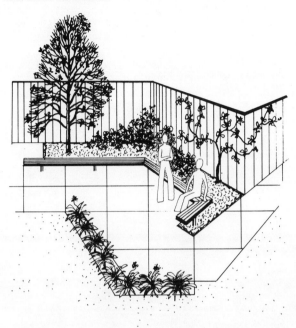

LANDSCAPE FOR BEAUTY

Landscaping should also be concerned with beauty—giving people pleasant sensory and emotional experiences. Satisfying physical needs—sun and wind control, play space, and work space—is not enough. How a human being reacts to his surroundings is equally important. Will he be excited by movement, intrigued by variety, soothed by quiet, stimulated by color, kept interested by change? A beautiful garden harbors secrets and surprises. It is never completely discovered. It contains sentimental values which change with the growth and age of the garden. There are more depths and dimensions of beauty in the garden to be lived in than in the garden to be just looked at. All the senses are involved. You react to what you touch, smell, and hear as well as to what you see.

Once you have your landscaping scheme, stay with it and let your garden mature. This doesn't mean that you are forever limited to the existing plants. Work within your general framework and experiment in plant selection. Look for new strains and new uses for old standbys. Consider shrubs used as trees and trees used as shrubs. Browse through your local nurseries. You may see some planting materials that you would like to introduce into your garden. Find out their growth requirements, then decide where and how you can most effectively use them in your garden. Be sure to coordinate any of these new plantings with the established ones.

Generous floor-level deck is a low-maintenance outdoor living room. Wide bench around edges of deck eliminates need for safety railing. Landscape architects: John Herbst, Jr. and Associates.

Midsummer garden color *is compliments of violas, marigolds, zinnias, and gloriosa daisies. Permanent plantings include tree roses at left and festuca in front. Concrete stepping stones form pathway around garden.*

Effective Landscape Planning

Making the most of your particular piece of land requires serious planning. Whether you are starting with property that is not landscaped or remodeling an older garden, first take stock of what you have and then decide what you would like.

The final test of a good landscape design is whether you are comfortable in your outdoor room and whether the outdoor room is used as it was intended to be. If you like casual outdoor living, chances are you will not be comfortable in a highly-manicured, formal garden. If you want to do extensive entertaining outside, your outdoor room will be more useful if you have a spacious deck or patio rather than an expanse of lawn. If you want to keep the main garden area neat at all times, then plan a separate area for the children where they can have their play equipment and expend energy without threat of harming favorite plants or trees.

There are some specific guidelines to follow that will help you most effectively landscape your home. This chapter deals with items to check, directions for putting tentative plans on paper, and hints on how to decide just what your landscaping needs are.

Easy-going, *attractive entry garden has raised beds of Natal plum, festuca, and nandina. Screens give privacy to streetside rooms. Pergola is both a decorative and a unifying element for the screens and walk.*

STUDY YOUR SITE

Your first step in home landscaping is to look at what you have before you plan for what you would like to do. Probably the two most important factors to consider are your climate and your plot of land.

The sun

The path of the sun and its intensity through the seasons of the year and the hours of the day affect the location and type of outdoor living area you plan and determine the kind of plants you grow.

If the number of warm, sunny days is limited, you naturally seek to develop areas where the sun can be trapped. You appreciate paved areas of concrete and brick that absorb the heat of the sun and reradiate it to increase the temperature near their surfaces. Where the amount of sun is limited, look to south walls to reflect extra heat for those plants that need it; avoid plantings that will shut off the sun in fall, winter, and spring.

If summer temperatures are high, you should attempt to temper the sun with overhead structures or screens of foliage and to minimize the amount of unshaded paving. Of course, the time of day you plan to use the garden will also influence what you do about the sun. Pavements

SUN AND SHADE ON A WEST-FACING PATIO

December 21, 11 a.m. Patio is almost completely in shade. For morning sunshine, the usual solution is to continue patio around corner on south side.

December 21, 4 p.m. Late, low western sun sweeps across patio into living room. If angle of sun is uncomfortable, block sun out with screens of tall shrubs or small trees.

March 21—September 21, 11 a.m. Sun is no problem in the morning. An overhead will increase amount of shade in early afternoon but will not block late afternoon sun.

March 21—September 21, 4 p.m. At this time, the western sun can be at its most disturbing angle. Both overhead and vertical baffles are needed to soften the sun's heat.

June 21, 11 a.m. Throughout the year, the west side of the house is in morning shade. If you use shade-loving plants on this side, grow those not disturbed by heat extremes.

June 21, 4 p.m. Try to intercept sun's rays by vines, trees, or structures to avoid the west wall's input of heat that reradiates into rooms of house after sundown.

too hot for afternoon use may be just the thing to take the chill out of the after-sundown air.

In North America, the sun is never directly overhead; this means that a tree or overhead structure will never cast all of its shade directly beneath itself. At midday, the sun is always somewhere to the south of a point directly overhead; at sunrise, it's always somewhere between the northeast and southeast points on your horizon; and at sunset, it's between the northwest and southwest points on the other horizon. How high the sun may be within this area at any particular time of day depends on the time of the year. The sun's arc is low in winter, high in summer (but never high enough to be overhead at noon).

To a small degree the sun's angle on any day also depends on how far north of the equator you live. But the effect of latitude makes only a comparatively minor change in sun angles between the Mexican and Canadian borders.

See the illustrations below for sun and shade patterns on a west patio and a south patio. Either a south or west orientation is perhaps the best location in the temperate climate zone because the sun provides warmth during the afternoon and early evening when you are most likely to use your patio. A north-facing patio will almost always be in the shade; this might be the ideal position for the patio if you live in an extremely warm climate zone. An east-oriented patio will receive morning sun

SUN AND SHADE ON A SOUTH-FACING PATIO

December 21, 11 a.m. Sun's arc is at lowest point, rays flood across south patio from midmorning to sundown. If patio is protected from wind, December sun will feel warmer.

December 21, 4 p.m. In cold winter areas, low winter sun on south-facing patio and rooms provides warmth. In mild winter areas, you may need some screening.

March 21–September 21, 11 a.m. Patio is in full sun, but 8-foot-wide overhang blocks sun from living room. Ideal in a mild climate; screening will be needed where summers are hot.

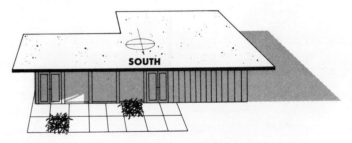

March 21–September 21, 4 p.m. It is difficult to get shade where and when you want it. For patio shade, use vertical screens on west side of lot.

June 21, 11 a.m. South patio is at its best when sun is high overhead, is good orientation where summers are short and extra warmth is needed in spring and fall.

June 21, 4 p.m. Late afternoon shade pattern leaves much of patio area in sun. Will be less shade from this day on. Correct sun's rays by plantings at west side of patio.

and afternoon shade. This situation is less desirable if you want to use the patio in the evening. However, this orientation might be perfect if you live in a warm climate or enjoy breakfast or brunch on the patio.

The wind

Make a careful study of the wind pattern around your house and over your lot. Too much wind blowing across an outdoor sitting area on a cool day can be as unpleasant as no breeze at all on a hot, summer day. The idea is to control the wind—block it by fences, screens, or plants, or modify its flow to suit your needs.

To determine your prevailing winds, notice the "lean" of the trees in your neighborhood. However, the direction of the prevailing wind around your house may not be the same as around the house next door. Wind flows like water—spilling over obstacles, breaking into several currents, eddying and twisting.

It is unlikely that anyone experiences exactly the same temperature as the thermometer at the weather bureau. When the weather bureau says that the temperature is 68°, it means that a thermometer in the shade, protected from the wind, reads 68°. If there is a 10 to 15-mile-an-hour breeze, a person in the shade in the breeze may feel that the temperature is about 62°. If the breeze is stopped and the patio is in sunlight, the person will feel a comfortable 75° to 78°. (See the following illustrations.)

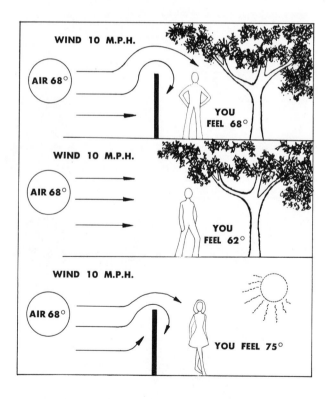

The cooling effect of a breeze becomes an advantage when summer temperatures are above 90°. In such cases, the path of the prevailing summer wind is an important design factor. You won't want to block the wind with obstacles like shrub plantings and solid fences. You may prefer vertical louvers to literally catch the breeze.

In checking the wind problem around your house, remember that the house itself is your biggest windbreak. However, it may need additions to be effective. In some cases, the wind spills over the house and drops on the patio. Remember, too, that a solid barrier is not always the most efficient. Wind washes over a solid fence as a stream of water would wash over a solid barrier.

You can use a fence to screen the wind. Leaving an open space at the bottom of a solid fence will give some wind control with maximum protection at a distance equal to the height of the fence. Adding a 45° baffle at the top of a fence increases wind protection because it eliminates the downward thrust of the wind; maximum wind protection is at a distance equal to slightly more than the height of the fence. Angling the baffle into the wind gives greatest shelter close to the fence. A louver fence gives the best protection over the greatest distance; reverse louvers direct wind into the area you want to protect. Lath fences diffuse the wind and give the widest protection—maximum protection is 12 feet away.

The seasons

The opportunities for outdoor living are, of course, greater in mild climates than in severe climates. However, completely comfortable outdoor living, hour after hour and day after day, is very rare. But each step you take to modify the climate increases the number of days you can use the outdoors.

If you pave an area immediately adjacent to the house, that area can be used between rain showers when the lawn would be too wet. If you control the breeze that sweeps across the patio, you can enjoy the patio in sunlight when air temperatures are much lower than the accepted 78° comfort temperature. A solid overhead allows patio use on rainy days.

When you consider your seasonal temperatures, think of all the days that you could use your garden if you did something about modifying the climate.

Your plot of land

Generally, property falls into one of two locations: an in-the-middle-of-the-block (interior) lot or a corner lot. The corner lot presents a difficult problem when you are trying for maximum private space. Compared to an interior lot where you give up the setback space on the front only, the corner lot may make you give up both side and front to the public. Depending on local ordinances, you may be able to use trees, shrubs, hedges, or fences to create additional private outdoor-use space between the house and the street. Although you may lose private space with a corner lot, you get a feeling of openness that you don't have in the interior lot.

No matter where your property is positioned, you will probably be faced with landscaping a rectangular, long and narrow, or pie-shaped piece of land. Following are some guiding principles to keep in mind when landscaping one of these parcels.

The *rectangular lot* is a rigid rectangle of clearly

defined space. The view of neighboring roofs and windows should be one of your prime considerations. Your back garden may be influenced by as many as five neighboring houses. When landscaping for privacy, do not be controlled by the definite geometric shape of your lot and plant just around the edges. Using curves can be one way to alleviate the rectangular feel of the garden. For ideas on how to landscape this type of lot, see pages 18-21.

The *long, narrow lot* should be designed to give the illusion of width or to at least prevent the eye from quickly measuring the narrow rectangle. Stay away from the tempting pattern of flower and shrub beds on either side and at the end of a lawn panel or your garden will feel like a hallway with a narrow green carpet down the center.

The *pie-shaped lot* with the narrow end toward the street can be the most desirable of all. It gives least space on the street and most space behind the house. Because of the large amount of back yard space, you can divide your lot into separate garden areas which if well-planned will hold together as a unit.

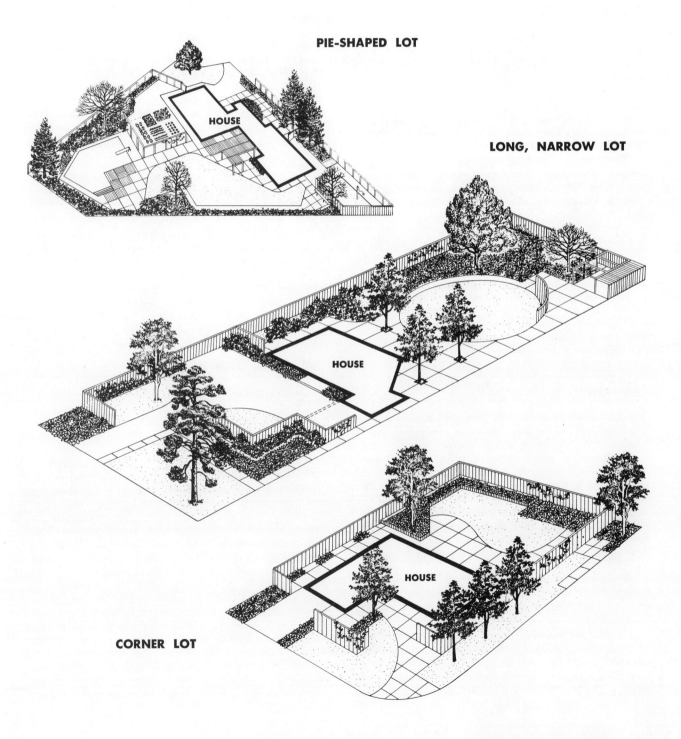

PIE-SHAPED LOT

LONG, NARROW LOT

CORNER LOT

EVALUATE YOUR NEEDS

The development of outdoor space for living can give the interior rooms an entirely new dimension. Check to see possible garden views from the windows of the house. Can a patio be built so that it is visually an extension of the living room? Would a kitchen patio be more usable? If indoor floor level is above ground, will the steps from house to garden be easy to negotiate? Would a deck at floor level make the living room larger and entrance into the garden easier?

You and your family

Planning a garden to fit the natural habits of your family is safer than to aim at changing those habits after your garden is built. If you do not like to be concerned with housekeeping, do not plan a garden that needs to be kept neat. If you have young children full of energy, plan a garden that can take their activities. A good garden is like a good house—it should accommodate the people who live in it, and it should be adaptable to their changing interests and needs.

Consider the kind of gardener you are. Do you garden because you must, or do you garden because you like to? If you are an experienced gardener and love it, do you have the time to give the garden the care it needs?

Do you plan to do the work yourself? Can you put together simple structures with hammer and saw? Does the prospect of laying bricks intimidate you? Will your older children help with the work? Is building, digging, paving, and planting your family's idea of fun?

At what pace can you work? Two factors are involved here: your budget and the time you can devote to installing your garden. For many homeowners working on their own, a reasonable garden installation timetable is two to four years.

Space requirements

You may want to include in your garden plan one or more of the following areas, depending on your family's needs and the amount of land available.

Patio area. A good-sized patio will give you a level surface on which to set outdoor furniture, container plants, and barbecue and will give you a place for entertaining or just relaxing.

Play areas. If you have young children, you can set aside space for a sandbox, play yard, or small portable swimming pool. You might also want to include a paved area for tricycles. Plan this area so it can be changed as the children grow up.

Game areas. If your family likes games, allow space for activities such as badminton, croquet, or even shuffleboard. A basketball hoop can be hung over the garage door, and the driveway can double as a basketball court.

Outdoor work area. If you like to do woodworking, painting, cabinet making, or other craft and hobby projects outdoors, include a work area. You might also want to include a separate work area for the children. If you install a clothesline, place it convenient to the utility area but visually removed from the patio, main garden area, or inside view windows.

Outdoor storage area. If you do not want to use your basement or your garage for storing garden equipment, plan an outdoor storage shelter. Set off in a corner of the garden, it can easily be camouflaged by vines or a planting of shrubs. Here you can put garden tools, lawn mower, wheelbarrow, paints, garden chemicals, peat moss, fertilizers, ladder, and lawn furniture.

Trash area. It's a good idea to have a place out of sight where you can hide an accumulation of trash until it can be disposed of.

Plant shelters. If you're a serious gardener, plan a lathhouse or greenhouse. Its size will depend on how much space is available and how many plants you want to grow.

Food garden. You may want to grow some of your own vegetables or even set up a small orchard. Very often a garden can provide both vegetables and fruit without sacrificing beauty or play space.

Water. Many people enjoy the sight and sound of water in the garden. A fountain or small pool is not hard to fit into the landscaping scheme, but a 16 by 28-foot swimming pool and the paving around it require a minimum of about 750 square feet

Utility connections

Consider the following when drawing up your garden plan. Will sewer pipes or a septic tank drain field interfere with tree plantings? Are water outlets placed so that future use is possible without cutting through lawns or pavement? Should there be a water faucet in the garden work center? A drain? What connections are there for sprinkler systems? If you plan to light the garden at night, do you have outdoor electrical outlets?

Soil and drainage

Successful gardening depends in part on the type of soil you have. Basically, the ideal soil is one that drains well but retains moisture and nutrients. If your soil is heavy (drains too slowly) or light (drains too fast), you can improve it with quantities of organic matter.

If your soil is shallow and underlaid with a compacted layer that is impervious to water and roots, you should remove the impenetrable layer. If this layer is too deep to dig out, bring in soil and garden in raised beds.

Before you begin landscaping, see how your lot drains. If your lot does not have a drainage problem, do not cause one by landscaping across the protective drain slopes and obstructing the flow of water away from the house. Large expanses of concrete or brick, unless properly installed, can choke off surface drainage. To avoid a drainage problem, you can bury drain tile underneath the patio area. Downspout water can also be channeled into this same drainage field instead of spilling across the patio. If a drainage problem occurs after the patio is constructed, you can divert water around the patio by digging a shallow trench along the edge and filling it with gravel. This ditch should slope to the drainage channels along the fence at the side of the lot. Still another way to handle drainage from a downspout is to use one of the canvas "hoses" sold for this purpose.

The area along the side fence is the main drainage channel for most homes. If water collects around a fence, there are several ways to handle the situation. You can put in a Japanese-style dry stream which turns into a real stream during the rainy season. Or you can plant the area with plants that are not harmed by water standing at their base.

Or you can try different tactics. Make a gravel path along the fence into a drain by cutting a V-shaped trench into the center of the path and then refilling with gravel; water usually stays below foot level. Or make an underground drain by digging a sloping trench 18 inches deep and filling it half full of gravel; cover the top and sides with polyethylene plastic sheeting and fill across the top with soil.

If you level or alter the slope of your lawn, be sure to make the center somewhat higher than the sides, or create a shallow channel or swale to drain off excess water. The most expensive and laborious but most permanent solution is to bury drain tile. Lay it on a sloping gravel bed, leaving a small space between tiles. Cover with rock, then with polyethylene plastic sheeting, and then with soil.

BASIC DESIGN PRINCIPLES

Before you put your plan on paper, look over the following examples which illustrate some basic principles of design.

• Most people recognize what are generally considered pleasant proportions and awkward proportions. If sizes and shapes are either too equal or extremely unequal, the sight of them is not pleasing. The following illustrations show this principle when applied to a section of the garden.

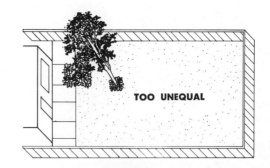

• The sense of proportion can't be plotted on a chart. One person may feel comfortable surrounded by free and easy space, while someone else may feel more comfortable in a small, heavily planted area. Space that is completely limited and defined seems relatively small; space that is partly limitless and partly closed seems large. When organizing space, you can use the knowledge that most people see orderliness in well-known shapes. The simplest shapes the designer can work with are the square, the rectangle, the triangle, the hexagon, and the circle. Many variations are possible just as long as the basic shape is recognizable.

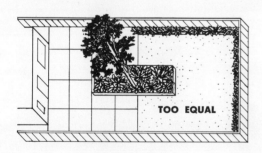

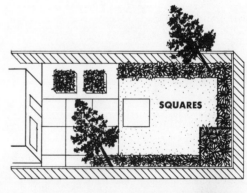

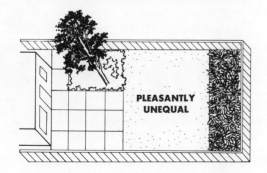

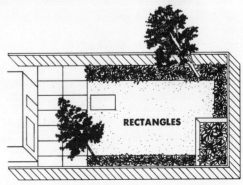

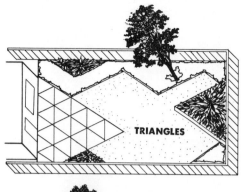

TRIANGLES

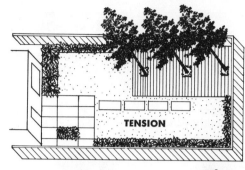

TENSION

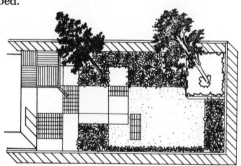

CIRCLES

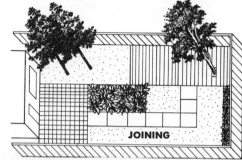

JOINING

INTERLOCKING

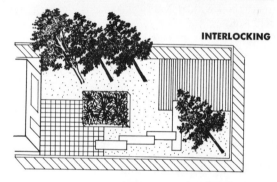

• The eye is not disturbed by a change if an easily recognizable shape carries through the main theme. A theme with variations creates a unified garden with variety and interest, without monotony. Below are two examples showing many variations of the basic theme being used—in paving, overhead, fence, lawn, and raised bed.

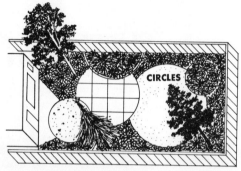

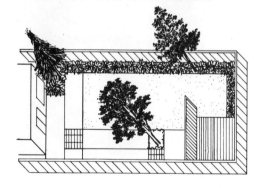

• In grouping shapes or masses, it is much easier to make them unified if you join or interlock the units rather than separate them and put them in tension with one another. In the following examples, the same units are arranged in three different ways.

• The safe way to impress the eye with a unified design is to create a rhythmic arrangement of units as a pattern. For example, here are the same units arranged with and without thought of pattern.

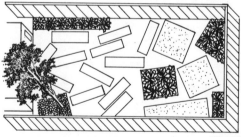

NO PATTERN

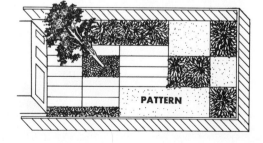

PATTERN

• Plantings and structures should be arranged to satisfy man's need for the feeling of shelter. However, to carry this to the point of where it prevents him from moving freely in the garden may give him a cooped-up feeling—the very feeling the small-house dweller comes into the garden to escape.

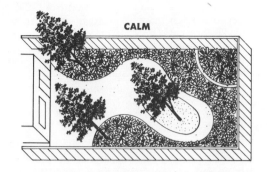

CALM

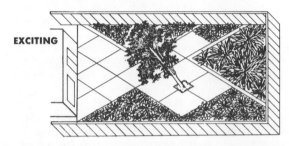

EXCITING

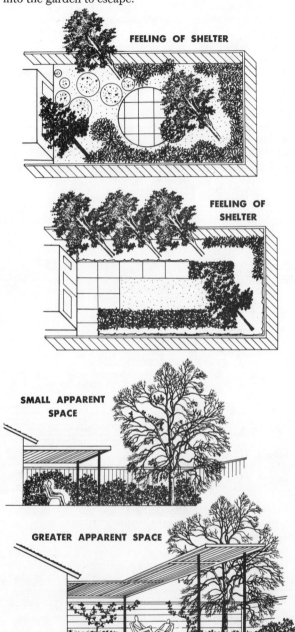

FEELING OF SHELTER

FEELING OF SHELTER

SMALL APPARENT SPACE

GREATER APPARENT SPACE

• Use the curiosity of man to sustain his interest. Create in your garden an invitation to explore what cannot be clearly seen—around a corner, behind a tree—by restraining parts of the picture from view. In the first illustration below, everything is seen at a glance from the patio; in the second, part is hidden, part is open.

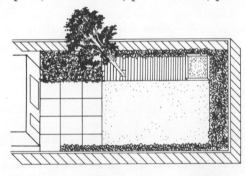

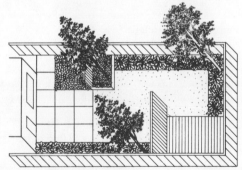

• Most people agree that curved lines are restful and natural; angular lines and zig-zags suggest speed, force, thrust. Here are two schemes composed of the same units. The first example is calm, the second is exciting. Fortunately the lines of the ground are not as dominant when you see them from eye level as they are when you look at a plan. Movement in the vertical elements can contradict the surface lines. If you use the so-called "exciting" plan, you can make its angularity disappear at eye level through the use of plantings.

Design pointers

In working out your own design, note some special devices used by landscape architects.

• Design generously, then count costs. You can get a feeling of luxury in the garden by only taking a step here and there beyond necessity. A 5-foot-wide brick walk will cost more than a 2-foot-wide brick walk, but it is more luxurious and by far more useful. A 10 by 16-foot patio may seem more than adequate to most, but a 12 by 20-foot patio gives that extra bit of room that can make the patio more delightful. In some houses, the usual step between the house and patio is only as wide as the door. Lengthen it and widen it and you not only go in and out of the house with ease, but you have a garden seat as well.

• Design boldly so that later plant growth will not completely erase your design. Design should make a strong and definite statement. Unless you lead from strength, growing plants will erase the design almost as soon as it is executed. What may appear too strong the first year is gentled and quieted by plant growth in the third year. The low wall, the wide mowing strip, and the raised bed are strong, built-in, permanent lines used boldly by the designer.

• Design can direct the steps of people, spread them out through the garden, bring them together, draw them to an entrance or an exit. For example, if the patio floor appears to be a part of the house, the edge of the patio will set the limit for movement of most people. However, if a wide path flows from the patio to another paved area in the garden—under a tree, perhaps—people will spread out through the garden. A second sitting area at a distance from the house gives everyone visual permission to move into the garden.

PUT YOUR PLAN ON PAPER

Your first practical step in getting your design on paper is to make a scale drawing of your lot by drawing a plot plan. The purpose of your plot plan is to show in measured relationship the limiting factors discussed in the previous section.

It would be helpful when drawing up your plan if you had either your deed map, contour map, or house plans. The deed map shows actual dimensions and orientations of your property. The contour map is very important for hillsides. It shows the exact shape of your site and may indicate property dimensions, streets, sidewalks, utilities, larger trees, etc. House plans show site plan, floor plan, elevations, how house is related to site, windows, doors, roof, utilities, hose bib connections, downspouts, footing details.

To begin, make a large map on graph paper to show in detail exactly what you have to work with. Draw to the largest scale the paper will allow—generally ¼ inch equaling 1 foot. This will be your base map. Show the following on your map. (The example used here is a rectangular interior lot.)

• Boundaries and dimensions of the lot.
• Orientation to the compass—indicate hot spots, shade areas.
• Direction of prevailing wind throughout the year.
• Location of easements that may affect your planning—underground telephone lines, trunk sewers (see deed map).
• Location of set back boundaries that may limit outdoor building. Check with your local building official about restrictions on such things as height and placement of fences, detached and attached structures, and ordinances regulating swimming pools.

• Location of utilities—water, gas, and sewer connections—and depth of each; underground electric or telephone wires; outlets on outside of house for water and electricity; sewer cleanouts; septic tank drain field; meter boxes.
• Location of your house—show all doors and windows and indicate from which room they open.
• Soil conditions—show location of fills, cuts. If you want, make test borings to determine character of soil (generally not necessary when remodeling an existing garden).
• Gradient—show contour lines; locate high and low points; indicate contours on neighboring property that will affect your planning by draining water into your garden; mark downspouts and indicate whether these are underground drains or sewer connections.
• Map existing plantings, particularly large, established trees; indicate names of plants, if known.
• Alongside plot plan, note the problems beyond the lot line such as good or bad views of neighbors' properties, hills, trees, telephone poles.

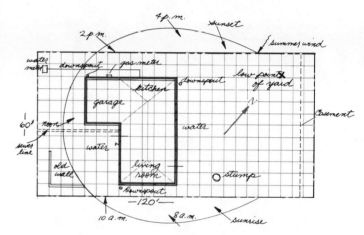

When you have in front of you all the physical restrictions and requirements imposed by your lot, bring out the check list you have made from evaluating your needs. Lay a sheet of tracing paper over the base map on which you have outlined the house and lot and do your planning on the tracing paper. If you make a wrong move, the base map is not marred.

Before you put your ideas down on tracing paper, you may want to get the overall feeling of your landscaping plan by drawing doodles. Doodles are helpful to many amateurs because by over-simplification they rule out minor details that get in the way of the basic plan. Most important, they do not have the serious aspect of a full-sized landscape plan. They are experiments in approach; they allow comparisons. Doodles come quickly. You can doodle a dozen plans in miniature while you are getting ready to put one final plan on paper. Just remember that the shape of your doodle plan should be in proportion to your lot.

General step-by-step planning

On a sheet of tracing paper placed over the base map, indicate the general areas you will need and their approximate locations; show where sun and wind protection will be needed.

Experiment with the relationships of space and plane and of form and line until the design suits you. Using the circle as the basic theme, indicate with a circle the separate areas you want—for example, lawn, storage, play, service, patio.

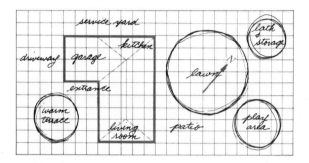

The next step is to define the specifics. Locate the entrance area and decide how you want to handle it. Do you want your front yard open or private? Do you want this area to be lawn, patio, or ground cover? If you want a patio off the living room, its location, and perhaps its shape, is predetermined.

However, the patio does not have to be attached to the house. If the patio is in a warm or windy spot, plan an overhead, trees, or fencing for climate control. Where

should the clothesline be? Where should the trash and garbage unit be situated so they are handy but hidden? Should a garden work area or growing area for cut flowers be included? How should the children's yard be handled? Should its surfacing be pavement, lawn, or bark? For the main garden area, what kind of grass should be planted? How should screening, either fences or plants, be used to visually separate the different areas of the yard? Should the garden be enclosed? Would fencing, plantings, or a combination of the two be most effective? How should the pathways be situated so traffic flows easily around the house and garden?

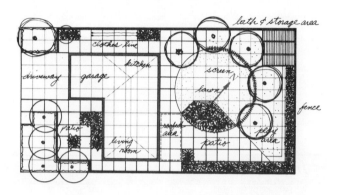

All of the above items were considered when this plan was drawn up. When perspectively illustrated, the plan looks like this.

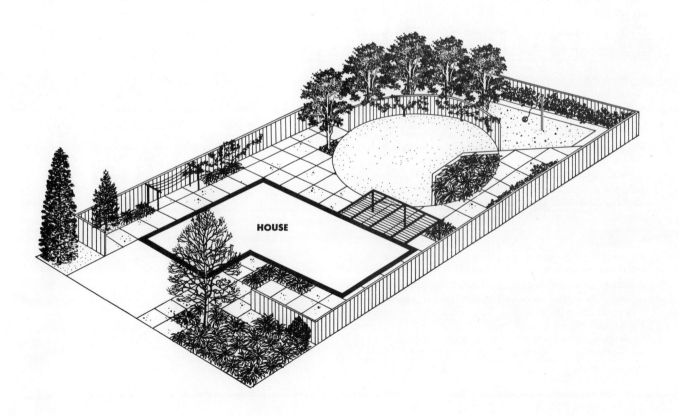

Planning with modular units

You can be more exact with your step-by-step planning if you work from a uniform module—in this case a rectangle or a square. Many people find it helpful to work with a unit of space, repeated again and again, like squares on a checkerboard or bricks in a wall.

Your module might be 3 by 4, 4 by 4, or 4 by 5 feet, or almost any larger rectangle that suits your needs. Using a rectangular module makes everything fall neatly into place; there's no question about what spacings to use or what sizes to establish.

If you decide to use a 4 by 5-foot module, all of your walks would be 4 feet or a generous 5 feet in width. Your patio would divide up into 4 by 5 rectangles. One or more of these might be an open 4 by 5-foot planting island within your patio area. Plant beds would be 4 feet across. A sandbox might be 8 by 10 feet, a raised bed 4 by 5 or 4 by 10 feet, a tree well 4 by 5 or 8 by 10 feet.

Besides a sense of order in your garden scheme, the module system offers other advantages. With the suggested dimensions, you have only 12, 16, or 20 square feet of paving to worry about at any one time. You can mix and pour concrete for just one rectangle at a time. You can lay one rectangle of bricks before you start another. If you're a little bit off with your brick courses, you can get a fresh start with the next rectangle.

Selecting your module. The length of the house wall adjoining the proposed patio can help you determine what size module to use. If the wall is 24 feet long, for instance, a 4-foot division in your patio paving would make 6 modules exactly fit your wall dimensions. If you work with bricks, you will avoid brick cutting if your module is an exact multiple of brick dimensions. Most professionals urge a module no less than 3 by 3 feet; amateur landscapers say a generous module saves work.

Designing the modular way. Using the same base map as described on page 18, here's how to work out a design using the modular system.

• Using a 5-foot-square unit, the entire lot was ruled off in 5-foot squares. The length of the house divides by 5, and the walks at the side of the house will be 5 feet wide.

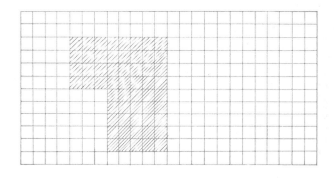

• For a paved area out from the living room, 3 squares were marked out, giving a generous width of 15 feet. For length, 6 panels or 30 feet were allowed, providing extra space for plantings.

• An overhead lath was included to protect a section of the patio from the sun and the wind. For added protection from the north wind, the north end was closed off with a fence.

• A raised bed with a seat wall was included, bordering the lawn area. A wood screen was added behind the raised bed for privacy. Room was left beyond the screen for a children's area or a service area.

• To get away from the rectangular feeling that this design was creating, trees for shade and wind protection were planted in a circular pattern.

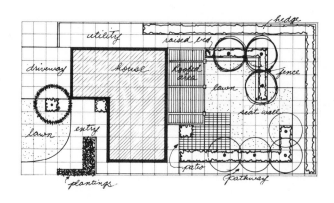

On the next page are four additional ways to design this same rectangular lot. In each example, space has not been designated for service, storage, or play. According to your habits, interests, and needs, you can locate these areas alongside the house or take some room away from the planted area. Each design involves a 5 by 5-foot module.

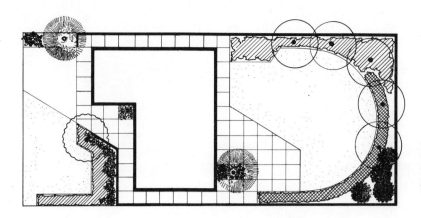

Spacious lawn curves around privacy screen and simple planting of trees. Angle of back patio and lawn is repeated in front with lawn and planting bed slanting off drive and entry.

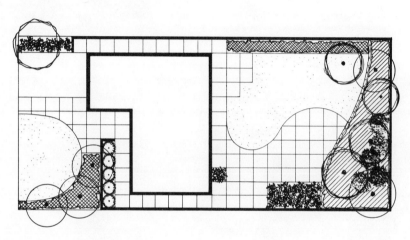

Free-flow of design is seen in U-shaped front lawn and trio of trees, curving back lawn, terrace, and planting of trees. Good-sized patio provides ample outdoor living space.

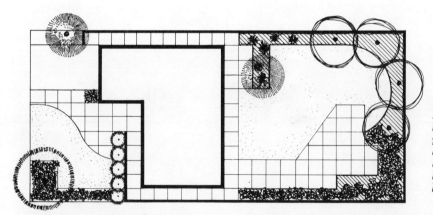
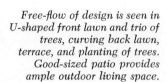

Different geometric shapes highlight this design. Back patio juts into section of lawn, as does a planting bed. Planting of trees complements curve of lawn. In front, free-flowing lawn has L-shaped bed.

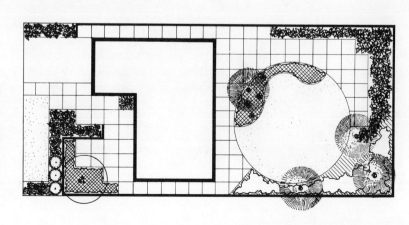

Circular lawn softens rectangular shapes of house and lot. Planting bed provides easy transition between patio and lawn. Perimeter plantings provide privacy, give backdrop to patio, lawn. Front area is combination of entry court, plantings, small lawn.

Cedar rounds *step through garden bed to small lawn surrounded by lush plantings. Protected patio is just outside living room.*

Spacious terrace *has brick flooring set in sand in running bond pattern, uninterrupted by headers. Cyperus alternifolius in containers, birch trees reflect in L-shaped pool. Landscape architect: Lawrence Halprin.*

Structural Elements for the Garden

Once your landscaping plans are on paper, you will know the location, size, and shape of your patio and pathways, how much and how soon privacy is needed, and to what extent the wind and sun need to be controlled. Your goal is to make your garden room as comfortable and as pleasant as possible. Therefore, it is important to select a surfacing material, privacy screens, and climate control devices that will be pleasing to your eye, that will fit in with your landscaping scheme, and that will be durable. And if you want to use your garden at night, outdoor lighting can easily be installed.

This chapter deals with the different materials that are available for paving, screening, sheltering, heating, lighting, and cooling the outdoor room. Carefully consider the characteristics of each material; then decide which one is best suited for your particular situation.

The actual installation of each material, whether it be pouring concrete, building a fence or overhead, attaching a heating unit to a patio roof, or putting in a garden fountain, is not covered here. For specific building information, see the Sunset *Garden and Patio Building Book*.

Wooded lot *was landscaped to suit naturalness of site. Rocks and native plants were used to make easy transition between cultivated garden, woodsy slope. Wide, unpaved stairs are outlined with concrete. Design: Robert Chittock.*

Bricks *in garden walk are set snugly on bed of sand, make an easy-to-clean and fast-drying surface.*

THE GARDEN FLOOR

When you think about garden pavings, keep in mind the basic idea of your garden plan. If you wish to create a mood of a woodsy retreat, concrete would be an intrusion. Wood blocks, tree rounds, stone, or exposed aggregate stepping rounds would be more suitable. If you want to use the garden for parties or for games, then smooth concrete would be a desirable finish. If you have small children and wheeled toys around, your surfacing material shouldn't be too soft, too rough, or too hard. In this situation, tile might be a good choice. If you want to invite the sun, use a material such as brick or concrete which holds the warmth of the sun. If too much sun is your problem, wood decking would be a better choice than brick or concrete.

Whether you do the labor or hire it done could influence your choice of materials. Many homeowners, if they are doing the work themselves, prefer brick because it can be easily handled. Your paving selection may also be influenced by your budget. Check with local building suppliers to find out prices of the different surfacing materials available in your locale.

Your paving selection need not be confined to one material. A combination of two materials is often more attractive than one used alone.

Bricks

Bricks as garden paving are handsome in almost any situation—from the curved sweep of an inviting patio to the straight pathways of a formal garden. And today you can choose a brick texture from rough to almost tile-smooth, a color from ebony to fawn. You can be an utter novice and still find bricklaying a challenge that needn't surpass your skill.

There are two basic kinds of brick—common and face. Most garden paving is done with common bricks because people like their familiar color and texture and their lower price. Face bricks are not as widely available as common bricks; however, they are being used more and more in garden paving.

Face bricks are more durable and more uniform in color and size—common bricks may vary as much as ¼ inch in length. They are less porous than common bricks and therefore will not absorb as much water.

Used brick, taken from old buildings and walls, is not often chosen for paving an entire area, but it can add a rustic look if set sparingly. To supplement the supply of used brick, manufacturers convert new bricks to used by splashing them with mortar and paint. Manufactured used bricks are not hard to find; their cost is slightly higher than common and the real used brick.

The exact dimensions of a standard brick (both common and face) vary depending upon the manufacturer and area in which you live. Standard dimensions are about 2½ by 3¾ by 8¼ inches.

Brick prices vary from area to area, ranging from 8 to 18 cents or more per brick. When you order, ask about delivery charges; they are usually low but are often not included in the quoted price. It is a good idea to pay a little extra and have the bricks delivered on a pallet; this prevents what can be considerable breakage in unloading.

Before you lay the bricks, make sure water drains away from the area you pave. If water is allowed to stand under the bricks, you may have problems with shifting and efflorescense (white deposits). In choosing the bond, or pattern, you are going to make with your bricks, keep in mind the degree of difficulty involved. Some bonds can demand a good bit of accuracy and brick cutting. (The jack-on-jack pattern—all bricks running the same way with all joints continuous—is the simplest.)

You can set bricks either in sand or mortar. Setting bricks in sand is easier for the beginner, and unless you live where the ground freezes, the bricks will be as permanent and as durable as bricks that are laid in mortar. Dry mortar is relatively easy to work with but will leave its mark on the brick. It is difficult to keep the mortar in the cracks, but the dry mortar method is a good process if you want a rustic, antique look to your paving. Wet mortar gives a clean, tooled, or shaped mortar joint between bricks.

Concrete

Concrete is one of the most versatile of all garden paving materials. The surface can be plain and smooth, or it can have a handcrafted, rough-textured look. Perhaps the most popular finish is exposed aggregate.

Because concrete is a flexible material, you can blend it with other materials and cast it into an endless number of shapes and forms. Circles, ovals, curves, and flowing lines can be handled more easily with concrete than with preformed materials. Where patterns of rectangles and squares are called for in a plan, concrete can be poured in forms to fit your specifications.

Concrete patios and walkways may be topped with any one of many colors. There are numerous earth tones from which to choose as well as various shades of green, yellow, umber, or red.

There are some disadvantages to concrete. A smooth, unrelieved slab will reflect heat and light into the house if the paving adjoins the house. Concrete is hard to the touch and cold in the winter, hot in the summer. Because it is porous, concrete shows stains.

You can buy concrete in one of the three following ways: dry bulk materials, transit mix, and dry ready-mix. Purchasing *dry bulk materials* is the cheapest way to buy concrete. You buy the required amounts of sand, gravel, and cement (the sand and gravel are already mixed together) and mix any amount that you want to use. However, you must have a place to store the sand and gravel, and the sack of cement must be kept absolutely dry. *Transit mix*, consistent and well-mixed concrete, is delivered to your door ready to set in place. No mixing equipment is needed, and the concrete can be prepared according to your specifications before delivery. You must be prepared to use the transit mix when it arrives, because the concrete could start to harden. Also, have adequate help in getting concrete off the truck or there will be standby charges. *Sacked dry mixtures* contain correct proportions of sand, cement, and gravel and are suitable for most home uses. Two sizes of sacks are available—60 and 90 pounds. All you have to do is add water, mix, and pour the concrete. This is

Concrete, wood, *rock, water, plants are effectively combined. Rectangular pads are used in different combinations—with water, mortared rock, loose rock, plants. Landscape architects: Chaffee-Zumwalt & Associates.*

ideal for patching old jobs or doing piecemeal work. Buying concrete this way costs about three times as much as the other two.

A concrete surface can have a smooth, an exposed aggregate, or a pebble mosaic finish. Your choices in finishes do not have to be rigid. You can drop a block pebble mosaic in a brick area, combine smooth stones with concrete, or play with contrasting colors and shapes, combining colored concrete, colored gravel, or brick.

You can achieve a cobbled effect by pressing large stones into a fairly stiff concrete mixture only to about half their thickness. If you wish to use this finish for an area that will receive traffic, push the stones into the concrete and level. Different effects can be achieved by the use of stones of different size, color, and shape. Or you may vary one module from the next.

Tile

Tile is the most finished-looking of all the garden paving materials. It is most effectively used on surfaces that are direct extensions of indoor areas, or under overheads where the house feeling rather than the garden feeling is wanted.

Tile comes in several sizes, colors, and shapes. Outdoor floor tile is rough-surfaced in contrast to the glazed varieties used indoors. The large, foot-square tiles are commonly known as patio tile and come in many colors including brick red. Quarry tile—9 by 9, 6 by 6—is obtainable in tones ranging from gray to brick color. Patio

Wood chips *cushion falls in the play area. Sandbox doubles as a landing place for whatever comes down the slide.*

a 1-inch thickness is essential to prevent cracking; thinner stones are set over a concrete slab.

For limited areas such as walks, where soil is stable and well drained, flagstones can be put down directly over the soil. Dig out the soil to a depth slightly less than the thickness of the flags and fit them in place. Fill joints with turf, or pack in some good soil and plant grass seed, or set in clumps of a creeping ground cover.

For a permanent surface, set flagstones in a mortar bed on a 2-inch slab of concrete. Work in small areas—set only one or two flags at a time.

Whatever method you use, avoid getting a pattern that is too busy or that has a quarry-like effect. Begin by laying all the stones loose, shifting them to please your eye.

Adobe blocks

Earth-colored adobe blocks are informal and soft looking, without glare or reflection. Several sizes of adobe blocks are popular for paving—8 inches wide by 4 inches thick by 16 inches long, 12 inches square by 2½ inches thick, and 12 by 4 by 16. A 4 by 4 by 16 block can be used as a veneer. Because dimensions vary slightly, adobe blocks are usually difficult to lay in patterns that call for snug fittings. Open joints, ¾ to 1 inch, compensate for irregularities.

Like brick, adobe blocks can be laid on a sand bed. Be sure that the bed is solid, stable, and quite level—when the blocks bridge a hollow or straddle a hump, they will crack when weight is put upon them. Joints may be filled with dirt, sand, or dry mortar. A dirt filling permits crevice planting.

When you buy adobe blocks, purchase extras for replacements—a few may develop flaws or disintegrate. It is difficult to match the color and texture later.

Unless there is an adobe maker in your locality, transportation costs will rule out this material.

Rock and gravel

Rock or gravel is a good surfacing material for paths, play yards, or service and storage areas. You can buy gravel crushed or uncrushed. Crushed gravel is manmade from larger rocks. The uncrushed kind is natural gravel, rounded by the action of glaciers, streams, and the sea. Gravel is commonly available in the following sizes (diameter in inches): ¼, ½, ¾, and 1½. A standard size for paths is ½ inch crushed. The smallest size obtainable is pea gravel, which is a rounded river-washed (uncrushed) type.

Rounded, uncrushed gravel is often used for the exposed aggregate finish. If it is loosely laid, the stones will roll underfoot. Crushed gravel packs better, and when rolled it makes a fairly firm surface. Gravel stands up best when put down over a more permanent bed of base rock or decomposed granite. But it will give several seasons' service when put right on the ground.

Sometimes gravel settles down into the soft earth so you may have to replenish it to bring it back to the desired thickness. Therefore, it's a good idea to order slightly more gravel than you think you'll need.

tile is not made to such close tolerances as quarry tile and consequently is cheaper per square foot.

There are several patio tile bonds from which to choose—from the basic square bond to a herringbone pattern. To save cutting or chipping, plan out surface requirements to stay within the dimensions of the tile you intend to use. Allow ¾-inch mortar joints for the large tiles, ½ inch for the small sizes. Patio tiles can be laid over a bed of sand or concrete. Quarry tiles should be laid over concrete, as they are liable to be chipped or broken if put down over soil.

Flagstones

If the feeling of the garden is entirely natural, flagstones, rather than the man-made pavings, may seem appropriate. The harder types of flagstone give a very permanent surface, and they will survive in winter where bricks sometimes fail. If you live in a severe-winter area, shop carefully because soft flagstones are sold in many yards. Flagstones should be scaled to the size of the area; in a heavily wooded area, play up the material's natural elemental qualities by using large scale blocks.

Slabs are irregular in shape; thickness most often ranges from ½ to 2 inches. For paving over a sand bed,

You can brighten up your landscape with decorative gravel—available in gold, black and white, white, gray and white, and maroon. Colored gravel comes in various sizes—small for walks, large for ground cover.

Red lava rock

Red lava rock gives an excellent color contrast to plants; however, it is too intense a color for large areas. It is not especially durable and may track; it turns to powder under heavy traffic. It is best used as an accent in small areas that receive light traffic.

Bark

Bark is a very natural surface both in walking "feel" and in color. It has a reddish-brown color, is soft and springy, and is not harmed by moisture. Since it scatters easily, it is best confined between header boards (see page 28). Use it on a path, as a generous cushion for a play yard, or in a part of a garden leading out to a natural, woodsy area. Use ½-inch pieces for walks or play areas; 1½-inch pieces for a ground cover.

Put the bark right on top of the soil for a path, but over 2 or 3 inches of gravel (for drainage) in a play yard. Buy the bark that is most readily available in your area—any kind will give good service.

Wood

Wood used as a paving material contributes warm color and soft texture to the garden. One or two rounds or blocks placed in a flower bed give you a place to step when you weed or water; several rounds set almost flush with the ground make an unobtrusive walk through the garden, or you can deck an entire patio with wood strips.

Wooden rounds are in good supply and are generally easy to find. They are usually a little more expensive than brick and require no special skills to set in place.

Wood will not last as long as concrete or stone. Three factors influence the length of time wood will last in the ground: the kind of wood you use, the ground you set it in, and whether or not you treat it. Wood decays most quickly in poorly drained, heavy, or very rich soil. Rounds last longest when set on a 1 to 3-inch-thick base of sand or gravel. Where summers are warm and dry, wood may warp or split.

Treating with a preservative will add years to the life of your rounds. To inhibit decay, paint (out of doors) with a preservative compound containing pentachlorophenol, brushing well into all surfaces twice, allowing the wood to dry for two weeks between applications, longer in cold or wet weather. Chemicals may be toxic to adjacent plants, so rinse rounds with water and let dry for a day before setting in the ground.

You can also buy rounds of pressure-treated wood. The pressure treatment gives the wood years of protection from insects or decay. If these rounds are not available, you can buy pressure-treated poles and cut your own rounds.

Wooden rounds *bordered by moneywort ground cover and Irish moss make pleasant path. Design: Richard Grimlund.*

Railroad ties *containing thickness of river stone make simple but effective garden steps. Design: James Leavengood.*

Wood rounds can become slippery when wet and, if used in the shade, may acquire a treacherous layer of moss. Rough sawn wood rounds provide good traction. Sharp sand spread on the surface also helps.

Lumber companies and some nursery and garden centers carry rounds or can get them for you. A few plywood mills saw butt ends of logs unsuitable for plywood into rounds. Small lumber mills, particularly those that split cedar shakes, will often cut cedar rounds to specific order.

Though 4 inches is the standard thickness of a round, you may want to go to 6 to 8 inches. The added thickness gives more stability underfoot. When blocks begin to decay in the center, dig out the poor wood and fill with concrete. For rough, nonslip treads, lay in pebbles before concrete sets.

Header boards

From a practical standpoint, it is impossible to consider paving without considering header boards. Header boards make a neat demarcation between lawn and plants, they keep grass and weeds out of plant beds, and they hold water within the root area of shrubs and plants. They also make handsome edging and division strips in brick, concrete, or other garden paving.

Redwood and cedar are the woods most often used, since they contain their own preservative. The most popular edgings are made of 2 by 4-inch lumber, either rough cut (2 inches thick) or finished lumber (½ inch thick). To prevent lumber from splitting, use galvanized box nails.

Paving tricks

By leaving generous open spaces for planting, you can make any paving material cover a much larger area and achieve the feeling of a bigger patio.

You can use 180 square feet of paving like this:

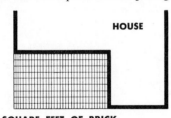

180 SQUARE FEET OF BRICK

Or, by adding 10 square feet of brick and two planting areas, you can double the size of your patio:

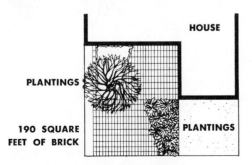

190 SQUARE FEET OF BRICK

Or, you can make the space apparently larger by tying it to the lawn and to a unit of planting:

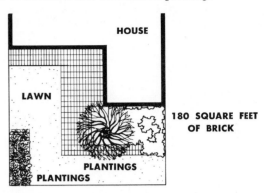

Or, you can enlarge the patio and still keep the feeling of brick by combining it with a less expensive material such as concrete:

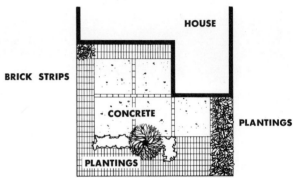

180 SQUARE FEET OF BRICK PLUS BRICK STRIPS

GARDEN SCREENS

You can use a fence, planting materials, or a combination of the two to enclose your outdoor room. If you want immediate privacy, a fence is your answer. The fence should be 6 feet high; anything less is useless as a privacy screen. There are several wood fence designs from which to choose—grapestake, slat, louver, board, basketweave, lattice, or solid wood panel. Select the style that will suit your purposes as well as fit in with your garden scheme.

Grapestakes, split from redwood or cedar logs, are lightweight and easy to install. They can be placed horizontally or vertically, in uneven pickets or in a frame. Although expensive, grapestakes are popular because redwood resists decay and because they weather to a pleasing gray. A *slat* fence, more formal than the grapestake, is good for controlling wind. The strips of rough-finished redwood or cedar can be nailed over a frame or set spaced apart or close together.

Louvered fences give you control over the amount of sunlight, wind, and privacy you will receive. Because of the interesting shadow patterns that change as the day progresses, do not hide the louvers under a vine or behind dense plantings. *Board* fences give maximum privacy, but they can also create a boxed-in feeling. To avoid this, you can vary the placement of the boards, leave the upper section of the fence open, or add panels of a pattern or texture. The *basketweave* fence uses a minimum amount of materials, and its interwoven design can be horizontal, vertical, or diagonal. This pattern is attractive on both sides, but if used in long stretches, it can have a dizzying effect. *Lattice* fences can be constructed of heavy or light lumber. Their grid-like pattern can be either a tight or open weave.

Solid wood panel fences go up quickly, but they require strong structural support. These panels insure complete privacy, and their flat planes make good display surfaces. A truly solid fence—one without any opening between boards or between the bottom boards and the ground—helps block out traffic noise from the street or any nearby freeway. Use either exterior plywood or hardboard. There are materials other than wood that you can use for panels that will withstand the weather. When using fence panels, the materials are more easily and less wastefully assembled if used in modules equal to the standard size of the material.

Asbestos-cement panels are made of a heavy, compact material that is fireproof and rot and rustproof. They come either flat or corrugated and in many colors (natural color is stone gray). As these panels are very heavy, they are hard to install. *Fiberglass* panels and *plastic* panels also come flat or corrugated and in many

colors. When correctly applied to a frame, these translucent materials will not break or scuff easily. They are especially useful in dark areas where a solid frame would cut off light. If plastic panels are exposed to the sun for a good length of time, the colors can fade and become dull. *Aluminum* panels come in many of the basic wood fence designs, and their baked enamel colors and finishes disguise the "aluminum look." They may corrode if in contact with damp soil, particularly if fertilizer has been used, and they can easily be damaged by garden tools.

Another way to enclose the garden is through the use of planting materials. A hedge or plantings of dense shrubs and trees will screen the garden. However, it may be several years before they are effective. (See pages 42-44 for a listing of hedge and border plants.)

You are not limited to either a fence or plants; a pleasant combination of both can be very effective. If you feel that your fence defines your property lines too rigidly, plant shrubs or trees to break up that feeling. Use trees to block out unpleasant sights or to frame pleasing views that rise above the fence line. To soften the lines of the fence, train a vine, such as ivy, for partial or complete fence cover. Or plant flowering vines, such as sweet peas or morning-glories, to add color and give relief to a section of a fence during the warm months of the year.

BASIC FENCE STYLES

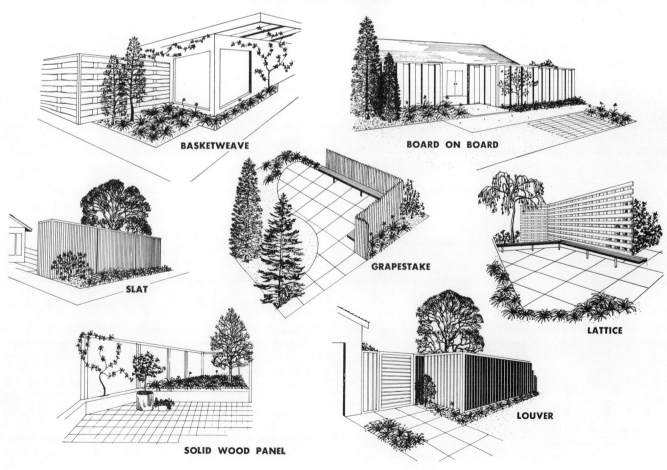

BASKETWEAVE

BOARD ON BOARD

SLAT

GRAPESTAKE

LATTICE

SOLID WOOD PANEL

LOUVER

Orange-flowered Streptosolen jamesonii *billow over fence; 4 by 4's set in horizontal pattern make handsome structure.*

Primulas *in redwood planters on fence bloom from late fall to spring, then yield to vine-like 'Swingtime' fuchsias.*

Fiberglass or aluminum screening

If you want to screen an outdoor room to modify the climate, design it for all-year use and all kinds of weather. The sides and top might have screened panels so as to open the area to maximum light and air. Then, during the summer, you could substitute panels across the top that afford some shade. If afternoon sun is a problem, you could use roll-down blinds of fiberglass woven to reflect the sun, reduce glare, and still not block your view entirely or interfere too much with air circulation.

On very hot days, you could fasten a lawn soaker across the screened panels on the windward side, and let the water trickle down the screening to cool the air blowing through the mesh. You could even install a ceiling fan or an air conditioner.

As more weather protection is needed, you could substitute panels of some translucent material on the weather sides, or the screening might give way to a fairly weather-tight enclosure.

On cool summer evenings, you can often raise the temperature within an enclosure to a comfortable level by covering the top and using some heating source. The screening tends to trap the heat by reducing air movement through the area and thereby makes the heater operate more efficiently.

Fiberglass and aluminum screening are the most readily available screening materials and can be found at building supply and hardware stores and in mail order catalogs. Both materials are fairly close in price and are available in several widths. However, for screened enclosures you probably won't be working with anything narrower than 4 feet. You can have the panels made or make them yourself.

Fiberglass comes in different colors—the darker colors have good see-through quality. There's little or no light reflection from the screening, so views out and in are sharper. Lighter color reflects light, so visibility in and out can be reduced. This can offer a degree of privacy and also have the advantage of reflecting solar heat and remaining cooler.

GARDEN SHELTER

An overhead of some kind will increase the usability of your patio by providing protection from the sun, wind, or rain. Your overhead can be structural or simply a tree. Many people feel a tree is the most beautiful and most natural roof of all. Depending upon the kind of tree you select, you have your choice of deep or filtered shade, high or low shade. One wide-spreading tree can eventually shade a 60-foot garden. Six small trees will give you shade more quickly and will do the job without dominating the garden. Remember, deciduous trees will drop their leaves.

If you need climate protection right away, you will need a structural overhead. If it is to be attached to the house, it should be planned to blend in with the style of the house. A freestanding roof allows for a more flexible design.

As with fences, you can combine the structural overhead with plantings. Vines, such as ivy or wisteria, can be trained along a wood-frame overhead for color and for more complete weather protection.

There are several types of overheads from which to choose—lath, reed or bamboo, canvas, fiberglass, aluminum, or louvered panels. A *lath* overhead, wood strips spaced apart (the distance can vary) and supported by beams and crosspieces, can be freestanding or attached to the house. It filters the rays of the sun and the force of the wind and lends itself nicely to a vine covering. *Reed* or *bamboo,* although not considered permanent materials, make an effective screen. They also provide more densely filtered shade and a more natural shade pattern than the lath.

Canvas, or a synthetic substitute, will withstand the sun, wind, and rain. However, the tightly woven texture does retard air movement. As canvas is lightweight, it requires less support and framing than a wood overhead. *Plastic panels* (both fiberglass reinforced and acrylic) are available in colors and textures. (Fiberglass reinforced also comes in corrugated sheets.) Translucent, they let in light (the amount depends on the color and texture) but keep out the rain. This material is light, shatter resistant, and easy to work with. *Corrugated aluminum,* available in many colors, gives complete overhead protection. However, it is noisy when the wind blows if not carefully installed, and it will expand and contract with heat and cold, loosening ordinary fastenings. Unless properly nailed on, it will leak around the nail holes. *Wood louvers* can be permanent or adjustable. Set permanently at an angle, they can block out the sun at certain times of the day. Adjustable louvers are superior as you can move the angle of the wood panels for better sun control.

TYPES OF OVERHEADS

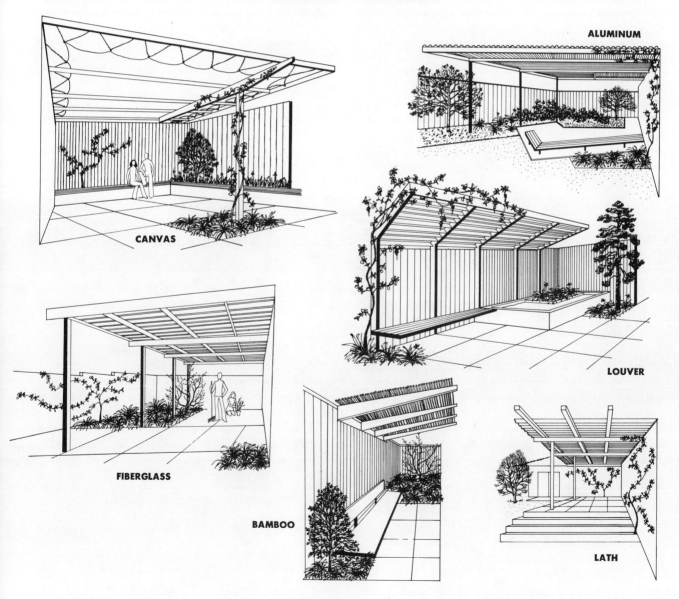

CANVAS

ALUMINUM

LOUVER

FIBERGLASS

BAMBOO

LATH

LIGHTING THE GARDEN

Garden lighting should be both functional and aesthetic. It should illuminate paths, walks, steps, and living areas for use at night as well as dramatize plant materials. Through the use of lights, you can change the personality of your daytime garden. You can emphasize a certain corner or area of the garden or favorite trees or plants by selective lighting. Night lighting can also bring to the garden interesting shapes, forms, and shadows.

With the adaptation of low-voltage lighting to use in the garden, outdoor lighting has become more popular. Low-voltage lighting is safe as long as the connector is properly installed. Even if a child removed the bulb from any 12-volt garden light fixture and poked his fingers inside, there would be little chance he would receive a dangerous electrical shock. If you inadvertently cut a 12-volt cable with a shovel or cultivator, there may be a spark but no shock. You can even go to the extreme of making connections underwater without feeling a tingle.

Another important feature of low-voltage lighting is the ease of installation. For low-voltage lighting, you need a transformer to reduce your 120-volt household current to the 12-volt current required. Most modern garden-light transformers simply plug into any handy and properly installed outdoor outlet. From the transformer on, the 12-volt wiring is simply buried a few inches in the ground, strung along fences, and run up tree trunks—without the need of conduit or protected cable, as would be necessary with 120-volt wiring.

You can install low-voltage lighting yourself. If you do not have the time, an electrician can install it throughout your garden at much less the cost than 120-volt wiring. And you can easily adjust or move the low-voltage fixtures as your needs change and your plants grow. (Leave slack in the cable to allow for any relocation of your garden fixtures.)

Lighting hints

Low-voltage garden lighting allows you to have low-key lighting. It is not only ample for illumination but extremely flattering to your garden, patio, and entryway. It lets you create shadows and silhouettes with plants, lets you accent architectural features—quite the opposite of placing floodlights under the house eaves. Floodlighting makes for strong illumination for a short distance away, but the light is flat and monotonous. You can see when you walk outdoors, but because of the glare your vision is limited when you turn around.

Creating the delightful low-key effect is a matter of experimenting with light in different places and different ways in your garden. With low-voltage equipment, you or your electrical contractor can simply string the wiring on top of the ground and leave it there for weeks, if necessary, until you decide exactly where each fixture should be placed.

Lay out your cable during the day but be sure to experiment at night—it is the only way to be sure of the effect. Try a light under a shrub, over it, behind it. Try one in a garden pool and also alongside it, reflecting on the water. The difference can be surprising, as can be the difference made by moving a light just a few inches.

Every garden is different, but here are some factors

Soft light *from unobtrusive fixtures mounted on stringers (left) washes over screen, plants at entry. Apricot tree (right) is lighted by two cylindrical fixtures buried in ground and positioned to highlight branches.*

to keep in mind when installing low-voltage lighting.

- Use six or more small lights throughout your garden rather than two or three more powerful lights.

- Place lights out beyond your patio. There, they create depth in the garden, and they draw insects away from the patio.

- Install separate switches for bright "activity" lights, such as near a barbecue or table tennis area, so they can be turned off when not needed.

- Consider using a few small lights on a fence or hedge, if needed, as a curtain between your garden and a neighbor's.

- When hanging lights in trees, place them above the bottom limb to create shadows.

- Be cautious in the use of color filters. A colored light can be handsome in a garden pool or waterfall, but it can destroy the nighttime beauty of flowers, shrubs, and trees.

- Light the hazards as well as the attractive features. You know where a garden step is, but guests may not. Use submersible fixtures in wet areas and garden pools, or else waterproof the connections thoroughly with a rubber seam compound. You can place any low-voltage fixture in water, but exposed connections will corrode and fail in time.

SOME LOW-VOLTAGE LIGHT FIXTURES

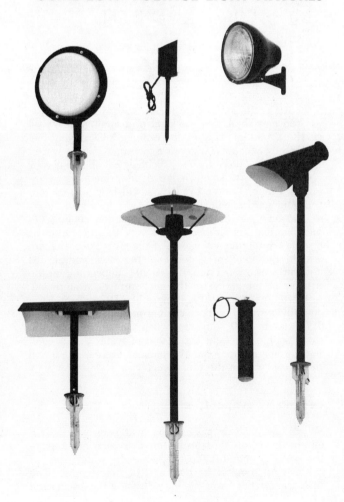

- Try placing a large mushroom light near the street end of your entry and smaller mushroom lights near the house to give an impression of depth and distance.

- Overall, try to feature the effects of your garden lighting, rather than the source.

HEATING THE GARDEN

If you live in a climate where the summer evenings are cool, there are several ways you can bring warmth to your patio. You can choose between a firepit, fireplace, floor heating unit, or infrared heater. All of the successful devices are based on radiating heat to the people rather than on heating the air.

If you decide on a floor panel or an infrared heater, remember that it's easier to warm a covered patio than one that is open to the sky. Sitting on an open patio at night, you lose heat to the sky—more to a clear sky, less to a cloudy one. You lose heat to moving air in proportion to the rate of movement. You lose heat to all nearby surfaces that are colder than you are. With an air temperature of 55° to 60°, the open sky may be equivalent to a ceiling with a temperature of 32° to 39°. Underneath an overhead, the ceiling will be the same as the air temperature.

Firepit or fireplace

In making a firepit, do not get it too deep. As soon as the heat source is below the level of the patio floor, it's of no value to those sitting around it. A raised pit is more effective than a sunken one. You are warmed by heat radiated from the walls of the raised pit as well as by the fire itself. If a low brick wall half encircles a firepit, heat will be radiated long after the fire dies down. If a concrete raised pit is faced with stainless steel, the radiation is intensified.

The firepit is not as efficient as the brick or stone outdoor fireplace. If your outdoor room can take a fireplace unobtrusively, it is a better source of heat. (Before constructing a firepit or fireplace, check local ordinances to be sure it is permissible.)

You can also use a portable barbecue as a source of heat. The greater the size of the brazier, the more heat will be radiated.

Floor heating

Radiant heating is probably the most effective—and the most expensive—way to heat the patio. Pipes are installed in a concrete slab or beneath tile or brick. A heated floor will make a 55° air temperature feel comfortable if there is no wind and if the patio has an overhead cover.

Infrared heaters

Gas-operated and electrical infrared heaters effectively warm the patio. Wall and ceiling units are available as well as freestanding, portable models. As these heaters

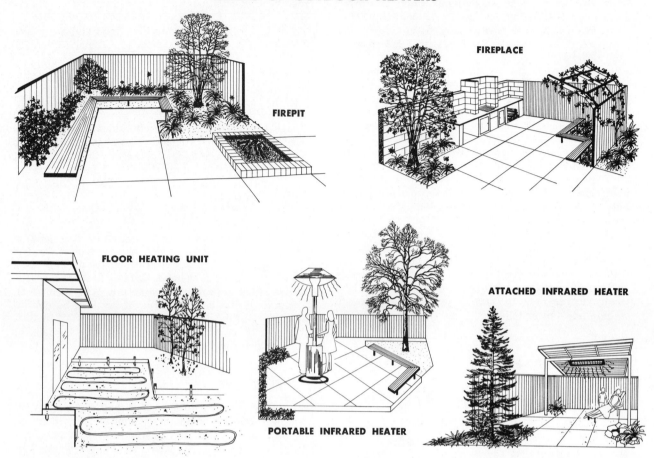

mainly emit infrared rays, reflecting them downward and out, they immediately and efficiently warm you, the furniture, and the deck or ground, rather than the outdoor air. However, they work best in a wind-sheltered area, because the objects heated by infrared rays will also warm the surrounding air to some extent.

The electrical infrared heaters range from 1,000 watts, 120 volts to 3,000 watts, 240 volts. The 240-volt unit produces about 10,329 BTU's per hour.

The largest gas-fired portable infrared heater is rated at 50,000 BTU's per hour, as much as a small house furnace. One will operate about 10 hours at full capacity on a 5-gallon propane tank. This heater requires no gas or electrical connection.

Similar semiportable infrared heaters are available that connect with a hose to a natural gas line or household propane tank. Other models are for permanent installation with rigid piping to a gas line. There is also a 25,000 BTU propane patio heater and still a smaller campground-patio model.

COOLING THE GARDEN WITH WATER

Water in motion gives the garden a feeling of freshness. And in hot, dry climates where soaring temperatures outside tend to keep you inside, water cooling can make a big difference in how you use the garden.

You may think that the sight of a small garden pool or the sound of a sprinkler running makes you feel cooler only because it suggests a mountain pool or waterfall. But it has more than a psychological effect on your physical comfort. A knowledge of the principles of cooling by evaporation and radiation will help you to control your garden climate.

However, in every scheme for garden cooling, remember that air temperature is only the measurement of how the thermometer feels. If the air is 90°, you can, with a sprinkling of water, cool the lawn and shrubs and surfaces around you 10° to 20°, depending on the dryness of the air. With the cool surfaces around you, a 90° temperature will feel more like 80° or less.

Obviously no outdoor cooling method will change a 100° day to a 70° day. But when the sun sets and you move within the sight and sound of water that is cooling garden surfaces and the passing breeze, you'll feel much cooler than the thermometer says you should.

Cooling by evaporation

When hot, dry air passes over water—on your skin, on the lawn, on the shrubs, on a terrace pavement—the water evaporates. To evaporate the water, the hot air uses up some of its heat and becomes cooler. The drier the air, the lower the humidity and the greater the heat loss through evaporation. This means that when a hot, dry breeze moves through water, it becomes a cool breeze. Of course, if the humidity is high, evaporation is slight and the breeze is not cooled perceptibly.

But wherever the humidity is low, you can reduce the temperature in your garden room by getting water into the air. Even a garden sprinkler will do this, but at the cost of very soggy ground and drenched surfaces.

For installations in a garden cooling system, look for spray heads that make a fine mist. There are many on the market and may be found at nurseries and garden stores. If your nurseryman does not carry them, or is unable to order them for you, check with commercial growers. They use mist sprays in propagating beds, in greenhouses, and in shade houses.

There are several types of spray heads available in various nozzle sizes. Some throw such a fine fog that they use only 3 gallons of water an hour. Look around your garden for places to use the mist sprays and foggers. They use so little water that they can be operated constantly without creating drainage problems. Try the mist sprays on vine-covered pergolas. For most efficient cooling, keep the vine damp on the windward side. For double-duty, install a mist spray over moisture-loving plants in a lath shelter.

Cooling by radiation

A hot object, surrounded by cold objects, loses heat to the cold objects. If the pavement under your feet is cooler than you are, you lose some of your heat to it. If the garden wall, or the leaves of a vine, are cooler than you are, you feel cooler when you are near them. Thus, to cool yourself, you should cool the objects around you.

This can be as simple as wetting down your patio floor with water or spraying the fence or vines or trees around you. The longer the surfaces can be kept cool, the longer you will be cool.

There are several ways you can have a small spray of water just where you want it. Black polyethelene tubing, available at hardware outlets, comes in coils; you can insert sprinkler heads into pre-punched holes. Or you can use a flat, plastic soaker with pre-punched holes. You can wind the tubing or the soaker over canvas roofs, along the fence, under lath, in the shade garden. Any masonry wall that absorbs water makes an efficient cooling panel when water is being evaporated from its surface.

Garden pools or fountains

Cooling your garden may not be a serious problem. You may want to add a garden pool or fountain for decoration or simply to bring water to the garden. Your pool or fountain can be simple or elaborate, large or small. It can be the focal point of your garden or an unobtrusive feature that is an integral part of the whole. When planning your pool or fountain, select a shape, planting materials, and additional accents such as stones that complement your garden design.

Brick fountain *has waterfalls, pool, island, bridge. Chrysanthemums add touches of color. Design: David Cousineau.*

Sprinkler system *is perforated plastic pipe hidden 2 inches below the top of the raised bed. Design: Tedd Wallace.*

Lacy *pinkish-white blossoms abound on supple branches of graceful Yoshino cherry tree, fall and rest on ground like unmelted snowflakes.*

Thick, green waves *of baby's tears surround and soften pathway of wooden stepping stones. Ground cover likes shade, ample moisture, and mild winter temperatures; does not withstand heavy traffic.*

Selecting Plants for your Garden

In planning a new garden or remodeling an old one, your first goal is to establish a permanent planting framework—one that will be independent of the come and go of seasonal color. Plants divide themselves into functional groups, such as hedges, ground covers, shade trees; from these groups you select the forms needed for your garden frame. You will want to choose plants that will be attractive to you throughout the year, regardless of how their appearance may change with the seasons. You will want plants that are well adapted to your climate, exposure, and soil conditions. Temperamental and tender plants should play secondary roles in your landscape scheme—so that their loss would not destroy the garden framework you have established.

Select plants with texture and foliage that are in good relationship to each other and to your garden's background. Build the basic framework with simplicity—remembering that everything you do with plants that have strong character or structure, or with seasonal color in bulbs, annuals, perennials, roses, or other favorites, will be more effective because of this simple background.

The charts on the following pages are a guide to selecting plants for your garden framework. The plants were chosen not necessarily for their individual qualities but for their effectiveness when used in a group and with other plants.

Chain fern *and agapanthus grow tall toward hanging branches of redwood trees. Baby's tears is ground cover, strawberry saxifrage is in bloom at right. These plants grow well in shady places, withstand heavy watering.*

PLANT HARDINESS ZONE MAP

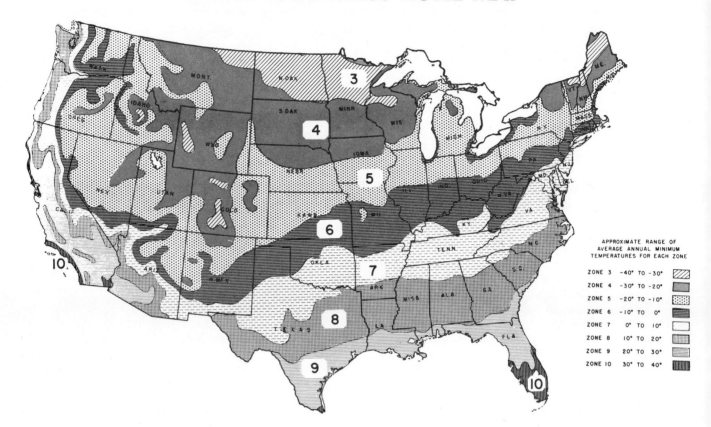

APPROXIMATE RANGE OF
AVERAGE ANNUAL MINIMUM
TEMPERATURES FOR EACH ZONE

ZONE 3 -40° TO -30°
ZONE 4 -30° TO -20°
ZONE 5 -20° TO -10°
ZONE 6 -10° TO 0°
ZONE 7   0° TO 10°
ZONE 8 10° TO 20°
ZONE 9 20° TO 30°
ZONE 10 30° TO 40°

The above plant hardiness zone map—devised by the United States Department of Agriculture—is used in countless nursery catalogs and garden books to indicate where plants can be grown. In the map's original concept, the reader was to locate on the map the climate zone in which he lived; then, if the zone number given for a particular plant was the same as, or smaller than, his climate zone number, the plant was judged to be hardy in his locale. In our listings, we have followed the standard method of hardiness rating; but in addition to indicating the coldest zone the plant will grow in, we consider its adaptability and usefulness in the warmer zones, and indicate all zones in which the plant is generally grown.

The limitations of the map are obvious. It is impossible to accurately map local variations in climate. Furthermore, a map based on temperatures only is misleading when considering plants which have special soil requirements; for example, plants such as rhododendrons, azaleas, and pieris require acid soil, but this soil will not necessarily be found throughout their range of favorable growing climates. In our lists we point out this localization within zones by noting plants that require acid soil.

In the following 13 pages, you will find charts which list plants in five different landscape categories:

• **Garden Trees.** These are the small to medium-sized trees which are in scale with most suburban gardens. A "shade" tree is one you can walk and sit under; listed under "patio" trees are those that are small, slender, or shrub-like and of interest when viewed intimately.

• **Hedges, Screens, and Borders.** This listing includes shrubs or shrub-trees which can be planted to form natural barriers varying from under 3 to over 12 feet high. Those that can be clipped into a more formal appearance are noted in the chart.

• **Basic Shrubs.** Here are a number of time-honored landscape favorites which are, as a group, neat and well-behaved. You will often find these planted in the front yard and near entrances. For other favorite basic shrubs with yet another landscape value, see chart of *Hedges, Screens, and Borders* on pages 42-44.

• **Plants to Cascade over a Wall.** Some of these are wide spreading shrubs, others are vines, but they all have the ability to drape gracefully over the face of a wall.

• **Ground Covers.** Included in this list are plants that can be lawn substitutes, vines which can cover a large ground surface, and spreading shrubs which look good when massed together.

• **Vines.** The range of choices goes from woody, structural vines to those that form dense, impenetrable mats. Those which are self-clinging are noted in the chart.

SMALL AND MEDIUM-SIZE TREES

NAME OF PLANT	EVERGREEN OR DECIDUOUS	FLOWERS	ATTRACTIVE FRUIT	DISTINCTIVE FOLIAGE	SHADE	PATIO TREE	CLIMATE ZONES								REMARKS
							3	4	5	6	7	8	9	10	
Acer ginnala AMUR MAPLE	D					•	•	•	•	•	•	•	•		Grown as a single tree or multiple trunked tall shrub.
A. palmatum JAPANESE MAPLE	D			•		•				•	•	•	•		Slow growth to 20 feet. Normally many stemmed, but can be trained as single tree.
Albizia julibrissin SILK TREE	D	•			•	•					•	•	•	•	Makes a beautiful canopy.
Amelanchier laevis SHADBUSH	D	•	•			•		•	•	•	•	•	•		White flowers in long drooping clusters before the leaves in early spring.
Arbutus unedo STRAWBERRY TREE	E		•	•	•	•						•	•	•	Attractive red-brown, shreddy bark.
Betula verrucosa EUROPEAN WHITE BIRCH	D					•	•	•	•	•	•	•	•	•	Often sold as *B. alba* or *B. pendula*. Lends itself to grove planting.
Cercidiphyllum japonicum KATSURA TREE	D			•	•	•			•	•	•	•	•		Light and dainty branch and leaf pattern. Single or multiple trunk.
Cercis canadensis EASTERN REDBUD	D	•		•		•			•	•	•	•	•		Profusion of small rosy pink flowers on bare twigs in spring. Excellent fall color.
Chionanthus virginicus FRINGE TREE	D	•				•			•	•	•	•	•		White flowers in lacy clusters. Deep yellow fall color.
Cladrastis lutea YELLOW WOOD	D	•			•	•	•	•	•	•	•	•	•		Leaves look somewhat like English walnut, bright green. Brilliant yellow in fall.
Cornus florida FLOWERING DOGWOOD	D	•				•			•	•	•	•	•		*C. f.* 'Rubra' is a longtime favorite for its pink or rose bracts. 'Cherokee Chief' has deep rosy red bracts that are paler at base.
C. kousa KOUSA DOGWOOD	D	•	•	•		•				•	•	•			Delicate limb structure and spreading, dense, horizontal growth habit.
Crataegus lavallei LAVALLE HAWTHORN	D	•	•		•				•	•	•	•	•		More erect and open branching with less twiggy growth than other hawthorns. White flowers. Large orange or red fruits.
C. oxyacantha ENGLISH HAWTHORN	D	•				•			•	•	•	•	•		Best known through its varieties: 'Paul's Scarlet', double rose to red flowers; 'Double White', 'Double Pink'.
C. phaenopyrum WASHINGTON THORN	D	•	•		•	•			•	•	•	•	•		More graceful and delicate than other hawthorns. White flowers. Chinese red fruits in autumn.
Cydonia oblonga FRUITING QUINCE	D	•	•	•		•				•	•	•	•	•	Yellow fruit and fall foliage. Will tolerate wet soil.
Diospyros kaki ORIENTAL or JAPANESE PERSIMMON	D		•	•		•						•	•		Spectacular large orange fruits hang on after leaves fall.
Elaeagnus angustifolia RUSSIAN OLIVE	D			•	•		•	•	•	•	•	•	•		Takes any soil. When pruned and trained makes picturesque tree.
Eriobotrya deflexa BRONZE LOQUAT	E			•		•						•	•	•	Bronze color of new growth lasts long before turning dark green.
E. japonica LOQUAT	E		•	•		•						•	•	•	Lawn or patio. Prune to shape. Big leathery leaves. Orange to yellow fruits.
Ginkgo biloba MAIDENHAIR TREE	D			•		•				•	•	•	•	•	Excellent yellow fall color. Plant only male trees.
Gleditsia triacanthos inermis HONEY LOCUST	D			•						•	•	•	•		Leafs out late, drops them early. Several varieties, all are thornless.
Halesia carolina SNOWDROP TREE	D	•	•			•			•	•	•	•	•	•	Grows 25-30 feet. Good overhead planting for azaleas and rhododendrons.

Small and medium-size trees continued

NAME OF PLANT	EVERGREEN OR DECIDUOUS	FLOWERS	ATTRACTIVE FRUIT	DISTINCTIVE FOLIAGE	SHADE	PATIO TREE	CLIMATE ZONES								REMARKS
							3	4	5	6	7	8	9	10	
Ilex altaclarensis 'Wilsonii' WILSON HOLLY	E	•				•				•	•	•	•		Shrub trained as small tree.
I. opaca AMERICAN HOLLY	E	•				•			•	•	•	•	•		Many selected forms.
Koelreuteria paniculata GOLDENRAIN TREE	D	•	•		•	•				•	•	•	•		Yellow flowers in upright clusters in summer. Bladder-like pods in fall.
Laburnum watereri 'Vossii' GOLDENCHAIN TREE	D	•				•				•	•	•			Yellow flower clusters 10-20 inches long.
Lagerstroemia indica CREPE MYRTLE	D	•				•						•	•	•	White, pink, red, lavender varieties. Available in shrub or tree form.
Ligustrum lucidum GLOSSY PRIVET	E			•	•	•					•	•	•	•	Round headed when trained to single trunk.
Magnolia grandiflora 'St. Mary' ST. MARY MAGNOLIA	E	•	•	•		•					•	•	•	•	Compact form of southern magnolia.
M. soulangiana SAUCER MAGNOLIA	D	•				•			•	•	•	•	•	•	To 25 feet when trained as a tree.
Malus CRABAPPLE	D	•	•			•		•	•	•	•				Many kinds varying in size, color, and hardiness. See box.
Nerium oleander OLEANDER	E	•				•							•	•	Needs training to become single-trunk tree, and constant sucker removal to remain one.
Nyssa sylvatica SOUR GUM, TUPELO	D			•		•				•	•	•	•	•	Copper red fall color, picturesque out of leaf. Very adaptable.
Olea europaea OLIVE	E			•		•							•	•	Willow-like gray-green leaves. Best as multi-trunked tree.
Oxydendrum aboreum SOURWOOD, SORREL TREE	D	•		•	•	•				•	•	•	•		Avoid underplanting with anything needing cultivation.
Pistacia chinensis CHINESE PISTACHE	D		•	•	•	•							•	•	Fall color in red tones. Not fussy about soil, water.
Pittosporum rhombifolium QUEENSLAND PITTOSPORUM	E		•	•		•							•	•	Very showy yellow to orange fruits and glossy, diamond-shaped leaves.
Prunus FLOWERING CHERRY	D	•				•				•	•	•	•		Many kinds are sold which differ in growth habit, flower color. See box.
Prunus blireiana BLIREIANA PLUM	D	•		•		•				•	•	•	•		Graceful. Leaves reddish purple, turning greenish bronze in summer. No fruits.
Prunus cerasifera 'Atropurpurea' PURPLE-LEAF PLUM	D	•		•		•			•	•	•	•	•		White flowers are followed by bronzy purple leaves. Fast growing.
P. c. 'Newport' PURPLE-LEAF PLUM	D	•	•	•		•			•	•	•	•	•		Purplish red leaves. Single pink flowers. Will bear a few fruits.
P. c. 'Thundercloud' THUNDERCLOUD PLUM	D	•	•			•			•	•	•	•			Dark coppery leaves. Flowers light pink to white. Sometimes sets good fruit crop.
Pyrus kawakamii EVERGREEN PEAR	E	•		•		•							•	•	Needs training to become a single-trunked tree.
Sophora japonica JAPANESE PAGODA TREE, CHINESE SCHOLAR TREE	D	•			•	•				•	•	•	•	•	Spreading tree, not particular about soil or water.
Sorbus aucuparia EUROPEAN MOUNTAIN ASH	D	•	•			•	•	•	•	•	•				Clusters of white flowers in late spring followed by clusters of bright orange-red "berries."
Styrax japonica JAPANESE SNOWBELL	D	•				•				•	•	•	•		Leaves angle upward from branches. White flowers hang down giving parallel tiers of green and white.

FLOWERING CRABAPPLES

Ornamental crabapples include at least two hundred named kinds, and new ones appear with each year's new catalogs. Longer lived than flowering peaches, hardier and more tolerant of wet soil than flowering cherries, the flowering crabapples are among the most useful of flowering trees.

Listed below are a few of the favorites. All are hardy to zone 4 with the exception of 'Dolgo' which is hardy in zone 3, and *M. sargentii* with a zone 5 rating. As a group they require less winter chilling than cherries and apples and therefore perform satisfactorily in all but the mildest winter areas.

Arnold crabapple (*Malus arnoldiana*), a fairly rapid grower to 20 feet and spreading wider, with long arching branches. Large fragrant flowers, 2 inches across, open pink, fade white. Small yellow and red fruits.

M. 'Dolgo', a large tree to 40 feet with willowy spreading branches. Foliage is reddish green and dense. Single white flowers are borne in great profusion in early spring. Cherry-like clusters of red, 1¼-inch fruits.

Japanese flowering crabapple (*M. floribunda*). Typical irregular, angular branching associated with flowering crabapples. Grows fairly slowly to 20 feet, spreading to 30 feet. Flowers, 1½-inch single, red to pink in bud, open white. Small red and yellow fruits are non-edible.

M. 'Hopa' is a vigorous fast grower to 25 feet with upright branches spreading with the weight of orange-red, ¾-inch fruit, excellent for jellies. Fragrant, single, rose red flowers.

M. purpurea 'Eleyi' is a graceful 20-foot tree with the typical irregular branch pattern. Attractive dark green leaves with reddish veins and stalks. Wine red flowers are followed by a heavy crop of ¾-inch purplish red fruits.

M. 'Red Silver' is a small 15-foot tree of typical crabapple structure with reddish or purplish bronze foliage. Wine red flowers and the purplish ¾-inch fruits are good for jelly.

M. sargentii is one of the best dwarf forms. Low, to 10 feet, and spreading wide. Fragrant, small white flowers in profusion.

FLOWERING CHERRIES

Use the Oriental flowering cherries as their growth habit indicates. All are good trees to garden under. The large spreading kinds make good shade trees; the smaller cherries are almost a necessity in Oriental gardens.

Hardiness and adaptability are variable. The hardiest (to zone 4) is the Sargent cherry (*Prunus sargentii*)— a tall grower to 40-50 feet or more with single blush pink flowers in clusters. Among the hardiest of the *P. serrulata* varieties are: 'Sekiyama' ('Kwanzan'), 'Fugenzo', 'Shirofugen'; all are hardy to zone 5. Also hardy in zone 5 are the Higan cherry and the Yoshino cherry discussed in the list below.

The flowering cherries are poor performers in wet soils and in warm winter areas. They need more winter chilling than is provided by zones 9 and 10, and parts of zone 8.

Autumn Higan cherry (*P. subhirtella autumnalis*): Grows to 25-30 feet and as wide with a bushy, round, flattened crown. Flowers, in autumn as well as early spring, are double white or pinkish white. In spring it blooms before the leaves appear.

Yoshino flowering cherry (*P. yedoensis*): Most of the famous cherries around the Tidal Basin in Washington, D.C., are of this variety. A fast grower to 40 feet with a 30-foot spread, with curving branches in a graceful open pattern. Flowers are single, light pink to nearly white. The variety 'Akebono' is smaller (to 25 feet high and wide) with darker pink flowers.

Here are 5 choice varieties of *P. serrulata*:

'Fugenzo' ('Kofugen', 'James H. Veitch'): A 20-to-25-foot tree spreading somewhat wider than high. Flowers, appearing with the new coppery pink leaves, are very large double pink, fading to light pink.

'Sekiyama' ('Kwanzan'): Fast growing to 18 to 25 feet with stiffly upright branches, forming an inverted cone. Flowers are double, deep rosy pink.

'Shirofugen': Grows to 25 feet with wide horizontal branches. Latest to bloom with a great display of double flowers on long stalks, pink fading to white.

'Shirotae' ('Mt. Fuji'): One of the earliest to bloom. A beautiful small tree, growing to 20 feet with spreading growth, arching branches. Flowers are double and semi-double, pink in bud, white when fully open, purplish pink as the flower ages.

'Shogetsu': A small tree to 15 feet with wide spreading growth, arching branches. Flowers are semi-double and very double, pale pink, often with white centers.

NAME OF PLANT	EVERGREEN OR DECIDUOUS	UNDER 3 FT.	3 TO 6 FT.	6-12 FT.	OVER 12 FT.	MAY BE SHEARED	CLIMATE ZONES								REMARKS
							3	4	5	6	7	8	9	10	
Abelia grandiflora GLOSSY ABELIA	E		•			•				•	•	•	•	•	Treat as perennial in coldest areas.
Acer campestre HEDGE MAPLE	D			•		•		•	•	•	•	•			Dense foliage. Responds to clipping.
A. saccharum 'Monumentale' SENTRY MAPLE	D				•					•	•	•	•		Columnar. Plant close for 20-foot-high screen.
BAMBOO	E	•	•	•	•						•	•	•	•	Choose from many. Vary in hardiness and height from 1½ to 50 feet. Yellow groove bamboo (*Phyllostachys aureosulcata*) is hardy to −20°.
Berberis buxifolia 'Nana' DWARF MAGELLAN BARBERRY	E	•				•					•	•	•	•	1½ feet high, 2½ feet wide. Good show of yellow flowers if not sheared.
B. julianae WINTERGREEN BARBERRY	Semi E		•			•				•	•	•	•		Holly-like leathery dark green leaves. Very thorny. Good barrier. Can be held to 3 feet.
B. mentorensis MENTOR BARBERRY	Semi E		•			•				•	•	•	•		Compact growth. Dull dark red berries. Stands hot midwest summers.
B. thunbergii JAPANESE BARBERRY	D		•			•				•	•	•	•	•	Dense foliage. Bright red berries. Also red leaf and dwarf varieties.
Buxus microphylla japonica JAPANESE BOXWOOD	E	•	•			•					•	•	•		Tolerates hot summers. Poor appearance in cold winters.
B. m. koreana KOREAN BOXWOOD	E	•	•						•	•	•				Slower and lower growing than Japanese boxwood. Hardy to −18°.
B. sempervirens COMMON BOXWOOD	E	•	•			•				•	•	•	•		Generally clipped to 3 to 5 feet but will reach 15 feet or more if not pruned.
B. s. 'Suffruticosa' TRUE DWARF BOXWOOD	E	•				•				•	•	•	•		Slow growing. Small leaves, dense form.
CAMELLIA	E		•									•	•	•	Choose vigorous upright growing varieties. Hybrid 'Flirtation' will take full sun.
Cotoneaster divaricata SPREADING COTONEASTER	D	•	•			•				•	•	•			Most often recommended for shrub border. Pink flowers give way to red fruit.
Cupressus glabra ARIZONA CYPRESS	E			•		•					•	•	•		Takes dry, hot situations.
Deutzia gracilis SLENDER DEUTZIA	D	•								•	•	•	•		One of the best dwarf shrubs.
Dodonaea viscosa HOP BUSH, HOPSEED BUSH	E			•								•	•	•	Takes any kind of soil, ocean wind, desert heat. There also is a purple-leafed variety.
Elaeagnus angustifolia RUSSIAN OLIVE	D			•	•		•	•	•	•	•	•	•		Gray foliage. Thrives in any soil, nearly every climate.
E. fruitlandii FRUITLAND SILVERBERRY	E			•	•						•	•	•	•	Especially valuable for seashore plantings. Silvery-like foliage.
EUONYMUS	E	•				•					•	•	•		Several varieties of *E. japonica* and *E. patens* are useful as hedges.
E. alata 'Compacta' DWARF WINGED EUONYMUS	D	•				•			•	•	•	•			Best when unclipped. Rich rose red fall color.
E. japonica 'Microphylla' BOX-LEAF EUONYMUS	E	•				•					•	•	•		Small leaves, compact growth, 1 to 2 feet tall and half as wide. Excellent edger.

NAME OF PLANT	EVERGREEN OR DECIDUOUS	UNDER 3 FT.	3 TO 6 FT.	6-12 FT.	OVER 12 FT.	MAY BE SHEARED	CLIMATE ZONES								REMARKS
							3	4	5	6	7	8	9	10	
Feijoa sellowiana PINEAPPLE GUAVA	E			•	•	•						•	•	•	Gray green foliage. Exotic fruit.
Gardenia jasminoides	E	•	•									•	•	•	Subject to periodic cold damage.
Hakea laurina SEA URCHIN, PIN-CUSHION TREE	E			•	•								•	•	Dense plant with narrow, gray-green leaves.
H. suaveolens SWEET HAKEA	E			•	•								•	•	Stiff needle-like leaves are stickery. Makes good barrier.
Hypericum patulum 'Hidcote'	Semi E	•				•					•	•	•		Deciduous in zone 7. Yellow flowers, 3 inches across.
Ilex cornuta CHINESE HOLLY	E		•	•		•					•	•	•	•	Without pruning, will grow to 10 feet. 'Burfordii' is the favorite variety.
I. crenata JAPANESE HOLLY	E	•	•	•		•				•	•	•	•		Looks more like boxwood than holly. Will grow to 20 feet. Many varieties.
I. glabra INKBERRY	E	•	•	•		•		•	•	•	•	•	•		Boxwood-like leaves. Low hedge or border. Dense. Slow growing. Hardy native.
I. opaca AMERICAN HOLLY	E		•	•	•	•				•	•	•	•	•	'Clarke', 'David', and 'Hedgeholly' are good varieties for hedges and screens.
I. vomitoria YAUPON	E	•	•	•		•					•	•	•	•	Accepts both seashore and dry interior conditions. 'Nana' is an excellent dwarf form.
Laurus nobilis GRECIAN LAUREL	E			•	•						•	•	•	•	Slow growing. Good container shrub.
Ligustrum amurense AMUR RIVER PRIVET	D		•	•	•	•		•	•	•	•	•	•	•	Hardiest of the semi-evergreen privets.
L. japonicum JAPANESE PRIVET	E		•	•	•	•					•	•	•	•	More shrub-like than *L. lucidum*, bushier.
L. lucidum GLOSSY PRIVET	E		•	•	•	•					•	•	•	•	Larger leaves than Japanese privet. Can be grown as small tree. Tall screen.
L. ovalifolium CALIFORNIA PRIVET	Semi E	•	•	•	•	•					•	•	•	•	Widely planted. Evergreen only in mild climates.
L. vicaryi VICARY GOLDEN PRIVET	E	•	•			•					•	•	•	•	Evergreen in warm areas. Dwarf growing. Bright golden foliage all year.
Liquidambar styraciflua AMERICAN SWEET GUM	D			•	•	•			•	•	•	•	•	•	Plant 6 feet apart.
Lonicera tatarica TARTARIAN HONEYSUCKLE	D			•			•	•	•	•	•	•	•		Many varieties, pink to white. Plant 5 ft. apart for screen.
Myrsine africana AFRICAN BOXWOOD	E	•	•			•						•	•	•	Red stems, tiny boxwood-like foliage. Good for clipped hedges.
Myrtus communis TRUE MYRTLE	E	•	•			•						•	•		Dwarf form most frequently used as low hedge.
Nerium oleander OLEANDER	E		•	•	•						•	•	•	•	Many colors. Wide spreading unless clipped.
Osmanthus fragrans SWEET OLIVE	E		•	•	•								•	•	Fragrant but inconspicuous flowers. A tradition for Southern gardens.
O. heterophyllus HOLLY-LEAF OSMANTHUS	E			•	•	•				•	•	•	•	•	Several varieties. 'Gulftide' has glossy dark green foliage.
Philadelphus virginalis MOCK ORANGE	D			•					•	•	•	•	•		Double white flowers.

NAME OF PLANT	EVERGREEN OR DECIDUOUS	UNDER 3 FT.	3 TO 6 FT.	6-12 FT.	OVER 12 FT.	MAY BE SHEARED	CLIMATE ZONES								REMARKS
							3	4	5	6	7	8	9	10	
Photinia fraseri	E				•	•					•	•	•	•	New growth coppery red.
P. serrulata CHINESE PHOTINIA	E				•	•					•	•	•	•	New growth bronzy.
Pieris japonica LILY-OF-THE-VALLEY SHRUB	E	•	•			•			•	•	•	•	•		Requires acid soil. Protect from sun and wind.
Pinus nigra AUSTRIAN BLACK PINE	E			•				•	•	•	•	•			Also windbreak. Dark green glossy foliage with very stiff needles.
P. resinosa RED PINE	E			•				•	•	•	•	•			Very hardy native. Dark green, flexible needles 4 to 6 inches long.
Pittosporum eugenioides	E		•	•	•								•	•	Glossy leaves have distinctive wavy edges.
P. tobira TOBIRA	E		•	•	•	•						•	•	•	Leathery leaves in whorls. There is a choice variegated form.
Podocarpus macrophyllus YEW PINE	E			•		•						•	•	•	Beautiful sheared screen.
Prunus caroliniana CAROLINA CHERRY LAUREL	E		•	•	•	•					•	•	•	•	Attractive foliage.
P. laurocerasus ENGLISH LAUREL	E			•	•	•					•	•	•		Heavy, rich green foliage.
Pyracantha coccinea FIRETHORN	E		•	•		•				•	•	•	•	•	Many varieties.
Rhamnus frangula 'Columnaris' TALLHEDGE BUCKTHORN	D	•				•		•	•	•	•				Set 2½ feet apart for a tight narrow hedge or screen. Can be held to 4 feet.
Salix purpurea 'Gracilis' DWARF PURPLE OSIER	D	•				•		•	•	•	•	•	•		Fine texture, blue-gray color effect. Can be kept at 1 foot high and as wide.
Santolina chamaecyparissus LAVENDER COTTON	E	•				•					•	•	•	•	Plant 2 feet apart for edgings and borders. Clip to 1 foot to keep neat. Gray foliage. Yellow button flowers.
Spiraea bumalda 'Anthony Waterer' DWARF RED SPIRAEA	D	•							•	•	•	•			Dwarf to 1½ feet or less. Makes low hedge or border.
S. vanhouttei BRIDAL WREATH	D			•					•	•	•	•			White flowers in summer. Fast growing.
Taxus cuspidata JAPANESE YEW	E			•	•	•			•	•	•				Many varieties.
T. c. 'Nana' DWARF JAPANESE YEW	E	•						•	•	•	•	•			Shrubby, spreading wider than high. Under 1½ feet.
T. media 'Hicksii'	E		•			•		•	•	•	•	•			Columnar.
Teucrium chamaedrys	E	•				•			•	•	•	•	•	•	Can be clipped any height up to 12 inches.
Thuja occidentalis 'Douglas Pyramidal' AMERICAN ARBORVITAE	E		•	•	•		•	•	•	•	•	•			Grows 8 to 15 feet.
Tsuga canadensis CANADA HEMLOCK	E		•	•	•		•	•	•	•	•	•			Prune and shear to any shape and height.
T. caroliniana CAROLINA HEMLOCK	E		•	•	•				•	•	•	•			Similar to above.
Viburnum opulus 'Nanum'	D	•				•		•	•	•	•	•	•		Highly regarded in cold areas.
Xylosma congestum	E-D		•	•	•							•	•	•	Height is easily controlled. May lose all leaves after sharp frost.

BASIC SHRUBS

NAME OF PLANT	EVERGREEN OR DECIDUOUS	LESS THAN 3 FT.	3 TO 5 FT.	5 TO 8 FT.	CLIMATE ZONES								REMARKS
					3	4	5	6	7	8	9	10	
Aucuba japonica JAPANESE AUCUBA	E			•					•	•	•	•	Many variegated forms are available.
Berberis verruculosa WARTY BARBERRY	E	•							•	•			Can be held to a neat 18 inches.
Chamaecyparis obtusa 'Nana' DWARF HINOKI CYPRESS	E	•						•	•	•	•		Very slow growing.
Choisya ternata MEXICAN ORANGE	E		•	•						•	•	•	Prefers light shade in all but cool-summer areas.
Cocculus laurifolius	E			•						•	•	•	Tolerates sun or shade, many soil types.
Cotoneaster horizontalis ROCK COTONEASTER	Semi E	•				•	•	•	•	•			Flat horizontal branches; widely used.
Hydrangea macrophylla BIGLEAF HYDRANGEA	D		•	•				•	•	•	•	•	Rounded plant with large bold leaves and thick flower clusters in white, blue, pink, or red.
Juniperus chinensis 'Armstrongii' ARMSTRONG JUNIPER	E	•				•	•	•	•	•	•		To 3 by 3 feet. More compact, smaller, than Pfitzer juniper.
J. c. 'Blaauwii' BLAAUW'S JUNIPER	E	•					•	•	•	•			Vase shaped about 4 feet high.
J. c. 'Fruitland' FRUITLAND JUNIPER	E	•					•	•	•	•			To 3 by 6 feet. Like a Pfitzer, but more compact.
J. c. 'Pfitzeriana' PFITZER JUNIPER	E			•		•	•	•	•	•	•	•	To 5-6 feet with arching branches to 12 feet or more.
J. horizontalis 'Plumosa' ANDORRA JUNIPER	E	•				•	•	•	•	•	•	•	To 18 inches, spreading to 10 feet. Plumy foliage. Plum color in winter.
J. sabina 'Tamariscifolia' TAMARIX JUNIPER, TAM	E	•				•	•	•	•	•	•	•	To 18 inches, wide spreading. Dense foliage.
Kalmia latifolia MOUNTAIN LAUREL	E		•	•		•	•	•	•	•	•	•	Needs acid soil. Glossy leathery leaves. Large clusters of pink and white flowers.
LANTANA	E	•	•	•						•	•	•	Many named hybrids differ in flower color and plant size.
Leucothoe fontanesiana DROOPING LEUCOTHOE	E	•	•					•	•	•			Needs acid soil. Good companion for rhododendrons, azaleas.
Mahonia aquifolium OREGON GRAPE	E	•	•					•	•	•	•		Leaves have spiny-toothed leaflets. Flowers in clusters; blue-black edible fruits.
Nandina domestica HEAVENLY BAMBOO	E	•	•						•	•	•	•	Graceful foliage, red in fall and winter.
Pachistima canbyi CANBY PACHISTIMA	E	•					•	•	•	•			Requires acid soil and shade. Used for borders and low hedges.
Pernettya mucronata	E	•							•	•	•		Small dark green leaves give fine-textured look.
Philadelphus lemoinei	D			•		•	•	•	•	•	•		Many named varieties with single or double white flowers.
Pieris floribunda MOUNTAIN PIERIS	E	•	•			•	•	•	•	•	•		Needs acid soil. Blossoms in upright clusters.
Pinus mugo mughus MUGHO PINE	E	•	•		•	•	•	•	•	•			Slow-growing. Shrubby, symmetrical.
Prunus ilicifolia HOLLYLEAF CHERRY	E			•						•	•	•	Must be trimmed to stay shrub size.
P. laurocerasus 'Zabeliana' ZABEL LAUREL	E	•						•	•	•			Branches angle upward and outward from base.
Raphiolepis indica INDIA HAWTHORN	E	•								•	•	•	Glossy dark green foliage. White to near red flowers.
RHODODENDRONS AND AZALEAS	D-E	•	•	•			•	•	•	•	•		See box.

Basic shrubs continued

NAME OF PLANT	EVERGREEN OR DECIDUOUS	LESS THAN 3 FT.	3 TO 5 FT.	5 TO 8 FT.	CLIMATE ZONES								REMARKS
					3	4	5	6	7	8	9	10	
Rosmarinus officinalis ROSEMARY	E		•	•					•	•	•	•	Aromatic grayish foliage. Blue flowers. Prune to keep neat.
Sarcococca ruscifolia	E		•							•	•	•	Excellent for shade; polished deep green leaves and orderly growth.
Skimmia japonica	E		•							•	•		Slow growing, dense, broader than tall. Good in shady areas, under low windows.
Taxus baccata 'Repandens' SPREADING ENGLISH YEW	E	•					•	•	•	•			Dark green, needle-like foliage. Long horizontal branches.
Ternstroemia gymnanthera	E		•	•						•	•	•	New growth is bronzy red. Needs acid soil. Also good as a tub plant.
Viburnum burkwoodii	D			•			•	•	•				Pinkish white fragrant flowers. Almost evergreen in warm climates.
V. carlesii KOREAN SPICE VIBURNUM	D			•		•	•	•	•				Long grayish leaves. Pink buds open white.
V. davidii	E	•								•	•	•	Neat, compact dark green. Turquoise blue berries are an added dividend.
V. rhytidophyllum LEATHERLEAF VIBURNUM	E			•				•	•	•	•		Dark green, 7-inch-long leaves with wrinkled surface. Slow growing.

RHODODENDRONS

The best rhododendron growing areas have a cool and humid climate, indicating influence by oceans or large lakes. In addition, winter low temperatures must remain above −25° F. for even the hardiest varieties. Considering these requirements, the most favorable rhododendron climates are found in coastal northern California, the Pacific Northwest west of the Cascades, and the area from Long Island to Philadelphia and south to Baltimore-Washington. With selection of proper varieties, two other favored territories are the Lake Erie shores of Ohio and Pennsylvania, and from New York City north to Boston. In other areas of the country—wherever winter temperatures are not the limiting factor—the culture of rhododendrons is more difficult because of hot and humid summers (Atlantic and Gulf coast states) and hot, dry summers and alkaline soil (central and southern California).

The easiest to grow and those adapted to the widest range of climates are the Catawba hybrids—the "iron-clad" group, all hardy to about −25°. These are the large leafed, large flowered, and fairly large growing conventional hybrids that are at their best in woodland settings, in large borders, or massed in a bank planting. Some of the best in this group are 'Catawbiense Album' and 'Boule de Neige', both white; 'Mrs. C.S. Sargent' and 'Roseum Elegans', pink; and 'America', 'Caractacus', and 'Nova Zembla', red.

Slightly less hardy (to about −10°) are: 'Cynthia', 'Mrs. Furnival', and 'Kate Waterer', dark pink; 'Dr. V.H. Rutgers' and 'Mars', red; 'Blue Peter', lavender-blue; and 'Purple Splendour', dark purple.

AZALEAS

Wherever they are adapted, azaleas can play important roles in woodland settings, shrub borders, mass displays, and foundation plantings. A vast array of hybrids are available, but most fall into these categories of both evergreen and deciduous types.

Gable hybrids. Hardy in zone 5. Although classed as evergreen, the winter foliage is sparse. Most varieties are of medium height and are heavy flower producers.

Glenn Dale hybrids. A variable group of evergreens in both hardiness and growth habit, they are at their best in zones 6-9. Many, many varieties are available.

Knap Hill-Exbury hybrids. Hardy in zone 5. These have the largest flowers found in deciduous azaleas, and they are carried in magnificent clusters. Colors range from white through pink and yellow to orange and red.

Kurumes. These are most useful in zones 6-9. Handsome evergreen plants generally are low growing, compact, and densely foliaged with small leaves.

Macrantha hybrids. Included here are plants that are sometimes sold as Gumpo, Chugai, and Satsuki hybrids; hardiness is about the same as the Kurumes. Most Macranthas are very low growing and useful as ground covers or in edgings. All are late blooming.

Southern Indicas. These are the garden azaleas famous throughout the deep south. They were selected for vigor and sun tolerance and may be sold as "sun azaleas." Most varieties take temperatures of 10° to 20°, but some are damaged even at 20°.

PLANTS TO CASCADE OVER A WALL

NAME OF PLANT	EVERGREEN OR DECIDUOUS	PERENNIAL	SHRUB	VINE	FLOWERS OR FRUIT	CLIMATE ZONES								REMARKS
						3	4	5	6	7	8	9	10	
Alyssum saxatile BASKET-OF-GOLD	E	●			●		●	●	●	●	●			Gray leaves, yellow flowers. May be killed in cold winters.
Arctostaphylos uva-ursi BEARBERRY, KINNIKINNICK	E		●		●	●	●	●	●	●	●	●	●	White or pink flowers are followed by pink or red fruits.
Asparagus sprengeri SPRENGER ASPARAGUS	E	●										●	●	Stems arch and droop to 6 feet if well grown.
BOUGAINVILLEA	E			●								●	●	One of the hardiest is sold under these names: San Diego Red, American Red, Scarlet O'Hara.
Campanula isophylla ITALIAN BELLFLOWER	E	●			●							●	●	Trailing or hanging stems to 2 feet long. Indoor-outdoor plant in cold areas.
Carissa grandiflora NATAL PLUM	E		●		●							●	●	Several named varieties are prostrate. Fruit is edible.
Ceanothus griseus horizontalis CARMEL CREEPER	E		●		●					●	●	●	●	Cut back any branches that grow upright.
Cistus salvifolius SAGELEAF ROCKROSE	E		●		●						●	●	●	Will take cold ocean winds, salt spray, or desert heat.
Cotoneaster adpressa CREEPING COTONEASTER	D		●				●	●	●	●	●			Slow growing, with ½-inch dark green leaves. Red fruit.
C. dammeri BEARBERRY COTONEASTER	E		●						●	●	●			Inch-long leaves on fast-growing plant. White flowers, red fruit.
C. horizontalis ROCK COTONEASTER	D		●					●	●	●	●			Will hang down 6 feet or more.
Euonymus fortunei 'Vegeta' BIG-LEAF WINTER CREEPER	E		●	●				●	●	●	●			Sends out long branches with side branches developing later.
Forsythia suspensa WEEPING FORSYTHIA	D		●		●			●	●	●	●			Drooping, vine-like branches.
Gelsemium sempervirens CAROLINA JESSAMINE	E		●	●									●	●	Long streamer-like branches cascade.
Hedera IVY	E			●				●	●	●	●	●	●	Grows down as well as up.
Iberis sempervirens EVERGREEN CANDYTUFT	E	●			●		●	●	●	●	●	●	●	For low walls.
Jasminum mesnyi PRIMROSE JASMINE	E		●	●						●	●	●	●	Large yellow flowers.
J. nudiflorum WINTER JASMINE	D		●	●				●	●	●	●			Slender willowy branches hang down.
Juniperus conferta SHORE JUNIPER	E		●					●	●	●	●	●	●	Will trail to 6 feet.
J. horizontalis 'Douglasii' WAUKEGAN JUNIPER	E		●			●	●	●	●	●	●	●	●	Trails to 8 feet.
Lotus berthelotii	E	●			●						●	●	●	Scarlet flowers stand out against feathery, silver-gray leaves.
Pelargonium peltatum IVY GERANIUM	E	●			●							●	●	Many varieties with bright, showy flowers. Light-green, ivy-like leaves.
Rosmarinus officinalis 'Prostratus' DWARF ROSEMARY	E		●		●					●	●	●	●	Endures hot sun and poor soil. Cascading branches will make a green curtain.
Sollya fusiformis AUSTRALIAN BLUEBELL CREEPER	E		●		●						●	●	●	Clusters of brilliant blue, bell-shaped flowers appear in summer.
Trachelospermum jasminoides STAR JASMINE	E		●	●						●	●	●	●	Glossy, 3-inch leaves and powerfully fragrant white flowers.
Vinca minor DWARF PERIWINKLE	E		●		●		●	●	●	●	●	●	●	Long trailing stems hang down.

GROUND COVERS

NAME OF PLANT	EVERGREEN OR DECIDUOUS	AREA LESS THAN 500 SQ. FT.	AREA MORE THAN 500 SQ. FT.	SUN	SHADE	CLIMATE ZONES								REMARKS
						3	4	5	6	7	8	9	10	
Ajuga reptans	E	•	•	•	•		•	•	•	•	•	•	•	Choice. Widely adapted.
Anthemis nobilis CHAMOMILE	E	•	•	•	•			•	•	•	•	•	•	Green carpet.
Arctostaphylos uva-ursi BEARBERRY, KINNIKINNICK	E	•	•	•	•	•	•	•	•	•	•	•	•	Prostrate, spreading and rooting as it creeps. Requires acid soil.
Ardisia japonica	E	•	•		•				•	•	•	•	•	Spreads by rhizomes. Leathery bright green leaves. White flowers in fall. Bright red fruits. Suggests holly.
Carissa grandiflora 'Tuttle' NATAL PLUM	E	•		•								•	•	Grows to 2 feet high, spreading 5 feet wide. Dark green glossy leaves. White flowers. Edible red fruits.
Cerastium tomentosum SNOW-IN-SUMMER	E	•		•			•	•	•	•	•	•	•	Spreading dense tufty mats of silvery gray. Snowy white masses of flowers in early summer.
Cotoneaster conspicua 'Decora' NECKLACE COTONEASTER	E	•		•					•	•	•	•	•	Low spreading.
C. dammeri BEARBERRY COTONEASTER	E	•	•	•				•	•	•	•	•	•	Flat, long trailing branches.
C. horizontalis ROCK COTONEASTER	D	•		•				•	•	•	•			Mounding.
C. 'Lowfast'	E	•	•	•					•	•	•			Thick, low, neat.
Euonymus fortunei radicans COMMON WINTER CREEPER	E		•	•	•			•	•	•	•	•		*E. f.* 'Colorata' has same spreading growth but leaves turn dark purple in winter.
Gaultheria procumbens WINTERGREEN, or CHECKERBERRY	E	•	•		•	•	•	•	•	•	•			Acid soil. Naturalistic planting.
Hedera helix ENGLISH IVY	E	•	•	•	•			•	•	•	•	•	•	Many varieties sold. Needs winter protection in zone 5.
H. h. 'Baltica' BALTIC IVY	E	•	•	•	•			•	•	•	•	•	•	Hardier than above.
H. h. 'Hahn's self-branching' HAHN'S SELF-BRANCHING IVY	E	•		•	•				•	•	•	•	•	Small areas, planters.
Hypericum calycinum AARON'S BEARD	Semi E		•	•	•				•	•	•	•	•	Rugged grower.
Iberis sempervirens EVERGREEN CANDYTUFT	E	•		•					•	•	•	•	•	Small areas, edgings.
IRISH MOSS, SCOTCH MOSS	E	•		•	•				•	•	•	•		Green and yellow-green carpets.
Juniperus chinensis sargentii SARGENT JUNIPER	E	•	•	•			•	•	•	•	•	•	•	Steel-blue, ground-hugging.
J. conferta SHORE JUNIPER	E	•	•	•				•	•	•	•	•	•	Light green. Good at seashore.
J. horizontalis CREEPING JUNIPER	E	•		•		•	•	•	•	•	•	•	•	Forms blue-gray mat 18 inches high.
J. h. 'Bar Harbor' BAR HARBOR JUNIPER	E	•		•			•	•	•	•	•	•	•	Plum color in winter.
J. h. 'Douglasii' WAUKEGAN JUNIPER	E	•	•	•		•	•	•	•	•	•	•	•	Turns purple in fall.
J. h. 'Plumosa' ANDORRA JUNIPER	E	•	•	•				•	•	•	•	•	•	Feathery, plum color in cold winter.
J. sabina 'Tamariscifolia' TAM JUNIPER	E	•	•	•				•	•	•	•	•	•	Favorite in warm areas.

GROUND COVERS

NAME OF PLANT	EVERGREEN OR DECIDUOUS	AREA LESS THAN 500 SQ. FT.	AREA MORE THAN 500 SQ. FT.	SUN	SHADE	CLIMATE ZONES								REMARKS
						3	4	5	6	7	8	9	10	
Liriope muscari BIG BLUE LILY TURF	E	•		•	•				•	•	•	•	•	Grass-like leaves; blue flowers.
Lonicera japonica 'Halliana' HALL'S HONEYSUCKLE	E		•	•			•	•	•	•	•	•	•	Good in tough situations. Invasive.
Ophiopogon japonicus MONDO GRASS	E	•	•	•	•					•	•	•	•	There is a variegated form; widely used zones 9, 10.
Pachysandra terminalis	E	•	•		•			•	•	•	•			Best in acid soil. Valuable ground-cover in shade and semi-shade.
Phlox subulata MOSS PINK	E	•		•		•	•	•	•	•	•			Late spring and summer color in a 6-inch deep carpet.
Rosa wichuraiana MEMORIAL ROSE	D		•	•					•	•	•	•	•	Good for dry banks, rocky slopes.
Rosmarinus officinalis 'Prostratus' DWARF ROSEMARY	E	•								•	•	•	•	Spreads 4 to 8 feet. Stays less than 2 feet high.
Trachelospermum jasminoides STAR JASMINE	E		•	•	•				•	•	•	•	•	Fragrant. Cut back to keep low.
Vinca minor DWARF PERIWINKLE	E	•	•		•		•	•	•	•	•	•	•	Widely used.

VINES

NAME OF PLANT	EVERGREEN OR DECIDUOUS	FLOWERS	DISTINCTIVE FOLIAGE	ATTRACTIVE FRUIT	CLINGS	NEEDS TYING	CLIMATE ZONES								REMARKS
							3	4	5	6	7	8	9	10	
Actinidia chinensis KIWI VINE, CHINESE GOOSEBERRY	D	•	•	•		•					•	•	•	•	Delicious edible fruit if both male and female plants are grown together.
Ampelopsis brevipedunculata BLUEBERRY CLIMBER	D		•	•	•				•	•	•	•	•	•	Brilliant metallic blue berries in late summer and fall.
Beaumontia grandiflora HERALD'S TRUMPET, EASTER LILY VINE	E	•	•			•							•	•	Needs rich soil, ample water, heavy fertilizing. Easter lily-like flowers.
BOUGAINVILLEA	E	•				•							•	•	Where frost occurs, give plants the warmest spot in the garden.
Campsis radicans COMMON TRUMPET CREEPER	D	•			•				•	•	•	•	•		Rampant growth, needs periodic thinning. Flowers grow in clusters.
Cissus antarctica KANGAROO TREEBINE	E		•		•								•	•	Vigorous but restrained growth.
C. rhombifolia GRAPE IVY	E		•		•								•	•	Grows well in sun or shade.
Clematis armandii EVERGREEN CLEMATIS	E	•				•					•	•	•	•	Needs constant pruning after flowering to prevent build-up of dead thatch.
C. jackmanii	D	•				•			•	•	•	•	•	•	Many hybrids with large showy flowers.
C. montana ANEMONE CLEMATIS	D	•				•				•	•	•	•	•	Vigorous and easy to grow. Massive spring flower display.

Vines continued

Name of Plant	Evergreen or Deciduous	Flowers	Distinctive Foliage	Attractive Fruit	Clings	Needs Tying	3	4	5	6	7	8	9	10	Remarks
Clytostoma callistegioides VIOLET TRUMPET VINE	E	•	•			•						•	•	•	Sun or shade. Needs pruning after flowering to prevent tangling.
Euonymus fortunei radicans COMMON WINTER CREEPER	E		•		•					•	•	•	•		One of best broad-leafed evergreen vines where temperatures drop below 0°.
Fatshedera lizei	E		•			•						•	•	•	Highly-polished 6 to 8-inch leaves look like giant ivy.
Ficus pumila CREEPING FIG	E		•		•								•	•	Rampant growth. Juvenile leaves are tiny and delicate; mature growth has large, leathery foliage.
Gelsemium sempervirens CAROLINA JESSAMINE	E	•	•			•							•	•	Vigorous but neat. Foliage pattern is not dense.
GRAPE	D		•	•		•									Bold foliage pattern. Adaptability varies according to variety.
Hardenbergia comptoniana LILAC VINE	E	•				•							•	•	Delicate foliage pattern, striking clusters of violet-blue flowers.
Hedera canariensis ALGERIAN IVY	E		•		•							•	•	•	Makes a dense cover. There is also a form with white and green leaves.
H. helix ENGLISH IVY	E		•		•						•	•	•	•	Will completely cover whatever it climbs on.
Hibbertia scandens GUINEA GOLD VINE	E	•	•			•							•	•	Restrained climber. Yellow flowers resemble single roses.
Hydrangea anomala petiolaris CLIMBING HYDRANGEA	D	•	•						•	•	•	•			Shrubby and sprawling without a support to cling to.
Jasminum grandiflorum SPANISH JASMINE	D or Semi E	•	•			•							•	•	Open growth gives airy effect. Fragrant flowers all summer.
J. nitidum ANGELWING JASMINE	E or Semi E	•	•			•								•	Not reliably hardy below 25°.
J. polyanthum	E	•				•							•	•	Strong growing and fast climbing.
Kadsura japonica SCARLET KADSURA	E		•	•								•	•		Fall and winter color comes from clusters of scarlet fruit.
Lonicera hildebrandiana GIANT BURMESE HONEYSUCKLE		•	•			•							•	•	Bold and heavy-textured with a semi-tropical appearance.
L. japonica JAPANESE HONEYSUCKLE	E	•				•			•	•	•	•	•	•	Rank growth needs control. Will form solid screen if grown on chain link fence.
Mandevillea laxa CHILEAN JASMINE	D	•	•			•							•	•	White, trumpet-shaped flowers have strong gardenia fragrance.
Parthenocissus quinquefolia VIRGINIA CREEPER	D		•		•		•	•	•	•	•	•	•	•	Clings to vertical surfaces or will double as ground cover. Good fall color.
P. tricuspidata BOSTON IVY	D		•		•					•	•	•	•	•	The ivy of the "Ivy League." Makes a fast, dense, even wall cover. Good fall color.
Passiflora alato-caerulea PASSION VINE	E	•	•		•							•	•	•	Striking, unusual flowers are white, lavender, and purple.
Phaedranthus buccinatorius BLOOD-RED TRUMPET VINE	E	•	•		•								•	•	Red flowers come in bursts throughout the year whenever weather warms.

NAME OF PLANT	EVERGREEN OR DECIDUOUS	FLOWERS	DISTINCTIVE FOLIAGE	ATTRACTIVE FRUIT	CLINGS	NEEDS TYING	CLIMATE ZONES								REMARKS
							3	4	5	6	7	8	9	10	
Polygonum aubertii SILVER LACE VINE	D-E	•	•	•					•	•	•	•	•	•	Very rapid growth but can be pruned to the ground yearly if needed.
Rhoicissus capensis EVERGREEN GRAPE	E		•		•								•	•	Will grow in full sun but roots need shade.
ROSE (climbing)	D-E	•				•									Many named varieties in various colors and flower sizes. See box.
Tetrastigma voinierianum	E		•	•									•	•	Good eave-line decoration. Glossy, dark green leaves may reach 1 foot across.
WISTERIA	D	•	•			•				•	•	•	•	•	Showy, pendant flower clusters. Plants need careful, early training.

CLIMBING ROSES

The popular term "climbing" is somewhat of a misnomer, as all climbing roses need some sort of support to climb against and tying to stay there; otherwise, depending on the variety, your climbing rose will sprawl on the ground or become a large, unruly shrub.

Several reasonably distinct types of roses are encompassed in the climbing category, and these are described here with good garden representatives listed. One other type you may run across is the "pillar rose"; these are simply the more restrained climbers (or, sometimes, a more exuberant bush) which will grow tall and narrow to no more than about 10 feet and which will flower when their canes are trained upright.

Climbing Hybrid Teas, Grandifloras, and Floribundas. Most of these plants are climbing "sports" of familiar bush varieties and bear flowers identical (although sometimes superior) to those on the bush forms. Depending on variety, some may be lusty growers to 20 feet; others will have only 8 to 12-foot canes. Most produce more blooms when canes are trained horizontally, as along a fence or wall or across the top of an arbor. Where winters are relatively mild (temperatures not lower than about 5° to 10°) these climbers need no protection, but in colder areas you will have to protect them, select the hardiest of this group, or choose from the list of large flowered climbers—many of which were bred for hardiness. In red, some of the best are: Cl. Carrousel, Cl. Chrysler Imperial, Cl. Crimson Glory, Cl. Etoile de Hollande, and Cl. Texas Centennial. Pink: Cl. Cecile Brunner, Cl. Charlotte Armstrong, Cl. Dainty Bess, Cl. Picture, Cl. Queen Elizabeth, and Cl. Tiffany. White: Cl. Snowbird and Cl. Summer Snow. Yellow: Cl. Peace, Golden Showers, High Noon, Paul's Lemon Pillar, Royal Gold, and Sungold. Multicolor: Cl. Mme. Henri Guillot, Cl. Mrs. Sam McGredy, Cl. President Herbert Hoover, Cl. Shot Silk, Cl. Sutter's Gold, Cl. Talisman, and Royal Sunset.

Large Flowered Climbers. Many of these are of the same bloom quality as the climbing hybrid teas and have hybrid tea in their background, but not all are as large flowered as the name would imply. Varieties such as Blaze, American Pillar, and City of York, for example, bear clusters of 2-inch blossoms. All, however, are exclusively climbing with no bush counterpart. Popular reds are: Blaze, Don Juan, Gladiator, Kassel, Paul's Scarlet Climber, Spectacular, and Thor. Pink: Aloha, American Pillar, Blossomtime, Coral Dawn, Dr. J. H. Nicolas, Dr. W. Van Fleet, Inspiration, Mme. Gregoire Staechelin, and New Dawn. White: City of York, Silver Moon, and White Dawn. Yellow: Doubloons, Elegance, Gold Rush, King Midas, Mermaid, and Mrs. Arthur Curtiss James. Multicolor: Joseph's Coat.

Ramblers. Quantity of flowers rather than quality of individual blossoms is the outstanding virtue of this group. Their growth habit is also distinctive: Instead of building up a framework of canes and blooming from the older wood (as do varieties in the two previous listings), ramblers bloom on year-old wood and send out numerous new canes after the spring flowering which will produce the next year's crop. These canes are thin, flexible, and long—20 feet is not uncommon. Most of these have one crop of blooms in the spring and have a tendency to mildew; in their favor, they generally are hardier than most other climbing roses. In red, try: Bonfire, Chevy Chase, and Excelsa. Pink: Dorothy Perkins and Tausendschon. Purple: Veilchenblau. Yellow: Brownell Rambler and Phyllis Bide.

Kordesii Climbers. Shrubby or climbing, depending on how you wish to train them, these German hybrids are rugged growers and will go through winter unprotected even in zone 4. Single to double flowers are produced in clusters throughout the blooming season. Some of the best are: Dortmund and Heidelberg (red), Sparrieshoop (pink), and Leverkusen (yellow).

Pathway *is brightened by blooming African daisies, hyacinth-flowering candytuft, Iceland poppies, petunias, stock, and marguerites.*

Shady deck *seems to be a secluded island in an oak and redwood grove, is really just a few yards from house (steps at right connect house and deck). Minimum landscaping of wild ginger preserves woodsy feeling.*

What Style Garden for You?

There may be a certain kind of garden that appeals to you. You may like one that abounds with blooms from flowering trees and shrubs, annuals, bulbs, and perennials. Or you may prefer the pleasant, even feeling that comes from an all-green garden.

Your goal may be a low-maintenance garden—one that can almost take care of itself. You will want to select plants that take little care and have ground covers and paving instead of a lawn. If you want to garden for a hobby, you will be more concerned with different varieties of plants, their usage and their growth habits.

Your gardening style may be dictated by your lot. If you have mature trees that cast shade, you should landscape with shade-loving plants. Attempting to grow sun plants in deep shade only results in leggy plants. If your site is wooded, landscape with plants that are native to the area; formal plants would look uncomfortable in a natural setting.

You can have a garden without having a piece of land. By placing containers of plants on a balcony or a window ledge, you can create visual excitement from inside or out.

Contrasting textures *of rocks, paving, ground cover, shrubs, trees add variety to landscape. Green mounds of Irish moss are soft and springy, take normal wear and tear of children at play. Design: Gene Zema.*

Gardening for Spring Color

Pink and white Darwin tulips, yellow daffodils, pink and white azaleas, white fairy primroses, pink rhododendrons, and fluffy ruffles of white evergreen candytuft all provide a spectacular display of spring color. Also in bloom in this 24-foot-wide, 50-foot-long garden are multicolored primroses, white hawthorn, and pink flowering 'Akebono' cherry. A little later, blossoms of fruiting quince add their shell pink color.

These spring-flowering annuals and bulbs were planted in late fall in planting beds filled wth imported top-soil, leaf mold, and redwood shavings; then they were fed monthly. Cobblestones were used for building raised beds as well as for steps.

A deck, partially enclosed with opaque glass for wind shelter and for privacy, forms the lower boundary of the garden and is an ideal spot from which to view the garden.

Deck design: William Wurster.
Consulting landscape architect: Thomas Church.

Delicate pink flowers, *graceful branches make 'Akebono' cherry tree an eye catcher. Large pots hold rhododendrons.*

Opaque glass *is wind and privacy screen, encloses deck at rear. Formally pruned Texas privets grow in white boxes.*

Strolling *down the lane, you pass a gardenful of spring-flowering azaleas, candytuft, primroses, daffodils, tulips.*

Entrance court *is enclosed, shaded by privet hedge, trees.*
Xylosma is hedge at right, star jasmine frames window.

Gardening the All-Green Way

Multiple use of a few kinds of permanently green trees, shrubs, and ground covers unifies the two gardens shown here. Broad-leafed evergreen plants complement the bold, clean-cut designs. The effect in both gardens is one of greenness, coolness, simplicity, and order.

The garden on the left uses evergreen plants to soften the glare from the large expanse of pavement. The courtyard and entrance court are enclosed with trimmed hedges of glossy privet (*Ligustrum lucidum*) and shaded by tree forms of the same plant. Also in the entrance court are boxleaf euonymus, star jasmine, and xylosma. Landscape architect: Guy S. Greene.

The all-green (and white) garden shown below has two aspects. Its street side is precise, crisply tailored, open, and sun-flooded. The rear garden is also perfectly groomed, but softer—with graceful curving lines, lush planting, and interplay of sunlight and shadow from high-branching trees. Landscape architect: Allan Himes Reid. Owner-designer: Alice Rydell.

Rear landscaping (*left*) *features greenery of boxwood hedge, azaleas, rhododendrons, ivy. Brick-enclosed planter contains olive tree, ivy. Front garden (right) is simply Algerian ivy, raphiolepis, star jasmine.*

Youngster *is enchanted by shallow L-shaped pool, bordered by river rock. Graceful vine maples arch over water.*

Maple leaves *cast shadow patterns on terrace, filter view of bridge and stairs which join different decks and levels.*

Shore junipers *almost conceal lakeside retaining wall. Benches provide seating on the exposed aggregate terrace.*

Gardening area *is designed for easy upkeep with paving, river rock, and undemanding but dramatic sword-leaf yucca.*

Gardening for Easy Care

This landscape was planned not only for expansive outdoor living and entertaining but also for low maintenance. There are no lawns to mow and edge, no garden beds to weed, no hedges to clip. Juniper, pine, vine maples, St. Johnswort, and yucca were planted for their strong design quality and for their ability to survive without coddling.

Little supplementary watering is needed, except for the flowers and ferns in pots and hanging baskets. Vine maples act as a leafy canopy of green to shade the terrace, yet their naturally small stature and open branching habit will never block the view from the waterfront house. A fountain jet splashes water into a shallow reflecting pool on the terrace.

This garden concentrates several outdoor living experiences in a small area by using several levels—terrace and decks all joined by stairs and bridges.

Landscape architects: Chaffee-Zumwalt & Assocs.

Gardening for a Hobby

This gardener wanted a garden for growing plants. He also wanted a private, comfortable, and attractive garden. A rough-cut cedar fence screens the back yard from an alley. At one point along the fence is a lath-house that also serves as an entry way. Its French doors take little space from the garden when opened.

The garden emphasizes design through a contrast of textures and patterns as well as a repetition of patterns. For example, an existing patio of tiles was extended by alternating concrete squares with Irish moss in a checkerboard pattern.

Plants make the patio a cool and inviting place to sit. Flower colors are predominantly pinks and oranges, chiefly from bedding begonias, fuchsias, impatiens, and zinnias. All were raised in the greenhouse.

Design: Thomas Batty.

Greenhouse *is the beginning place for garden plants and a growing area for cactus and tender tropical plants.*

Effective combination *of leaf form and texture includes meadow rue, Bethlehem sage, rhododendrons, hosta, native ferns.*

Tile patio *is quiet, protected part of the garden. Plants include large-leafed fuchsia, rose, ivy geranium, and iris.*

Checkerboard surface *is foot-square concrete pads alternating with Irish moss. Hydrangea softens house corner.*

Gardening in Deep Shade

Plants that thrive in heavy shade were selected to grow in this garden under a grove of tall, bigleaf (or Oregon) maple trees.

Continual experiments with plant combinations are carried on in an attempt to provide the best possible growing conditions for the plants. At the same time, plants are used to support rather than compete with one another. In one bed, for example, *Coptis laciniata* makes a lacy edge for mounds of *Epimedium*, at the same time hiding the *Epimedium's* legginess. The two foliages contrast color and shape beautifully, yet neither plant tries to overcome the other.

Making a garden grow under bigleaf maples brings its own special problems. Suckers on the big trees must be cleaned out every year, or the heavy waterloaded suckers may break off with the brittle old wood, damaging plants growing below. Tree roots tend to clog the soil for many feet in every direction, so they should be hacked off occasionally.

Design: Alton H. DuFlon.

Native ferns *bordering narrow brick pathway which leads to entry create an effect like a forest glade.*

Railroad ties *form streetside curb. Between ties and fence and beneath vine maples grow native sword ferns.*

Deer fern *and low-growing Mahonia crowd each other in rock crevices above violet leaves which form low ground cover.*

Towering *Oregon or bigleaf maples give lot established and restful appearance, deep shade, and woodsy feeling.*

Bamboo hedge *screens house from road; St. Johnswort is ground cover. Log sections keep cars off unpaved sidewalk.*

Clearing *lets light into side of house. Metal rake removes fallen leaves from ⅝-inch gravel contained in wood frames.*

Gardening with Native Plants

This garden proves you don't have to destroy surrounding woods when you build a house and landscape around it. Instead, you can enhance the woodland and extend it right up to the house with a garden that uses mostly native and evergreen plants.

This remarkably natural garden was created by planting many rhododendrons, vine maples, ferns, and other plants native to the area. Many of the plants came either from friends or from the surrounding woods. A quiet pool and bridge, rock arrangements, and several small stone lanterns complement the natural plantings.

The focal point of the garden is the pool area. After a concrete shell was poured, small pebbles and river stones were individually pressed into it to give the pool a natural look. The pool water is drained and replaced frequently to keep it clear.

At the pool's edges, river grass, bear grass, maidenhair and sword ferns, salal, bergenia, and Japanese iris grow. Moss gathered from the woods and Irish moss grow in spaces left between smooth, flat stones forming the pool's banks.

The garden uses five varieties of bamboo. Near the pool, dwarf bamboo is used as a low ground cover and landscape plant. Taller golden bamboo and black bamboo grow around the pool in clumps. A thick, 6½-foot-high hedge of metake bamboo gives privacy to the pool area and house, screening it from the road. Creeping St. Johnswort grows low in front, making a natural transition between bamboo and sidewalk.

To integrate the woods and the garden, giant timber bamboo was planted among the woods bordering the graveled clearing. The bamboo stays green in winter when many of the forest trees lose their leaves.

Design: William Bernard.

Natural-looking *garden pool with bridge is ringed by vine maple, bamboo, small conifer, rhododendron, and bergenia.*

Gardening for Outdoor Living

Double glass doors from the dining room open onto this spacious terrace designed for outdoor living. Slightly raised from the lawn area, the exposed aggregate terrace is at floor level of the house, making it possible to wheel dishes and food directly from house to patio.

Around three sides of the outdoor room are slat benches 4 feet wide—broad enough for sun-bathing—that also serve as railings around the edge of the terrace. In the middle of the terrace is a circular sunken firepit. A fire here makes it pleasant even in chilly weather.

The outdoor lamp at one corner of the terrace has a hood in scale with the outdoor setting. It stands nearly 3 feet above the bench on four 3 by 3-inch redwood posts. The four sides are horizontal slats made of 1 by 2-inch pieces of redwood spaced ½ inch apart. The light tops a post that is set in concrete.

Landscape architect: Moritz Kundig Associates.

Low benches *around terrace are 4 feet wide, useful for buffet suppers, also for seating or spreading sleeping bag.*

Outdoor living room *is spacious exposed aggregate terrace at floor level of house just off dining room. Terrace has sunken firepit, 4-foot-wide built-in slat benches, and a hooded lamp.*

Gardening without a Garden

Window boxes give you an opportunity to have a garden without having a plot of land. These boxes not only brighten up the view from inside, but liven up the façade of a residential or commercial building.

The window boxes shown here were made from all-heart redwood. The inside of the boxes were painted with copper naphthanate and the outside with pentachlorophenol—to prevent decay and to keep the redwood looking pink.

Plants for these boxes were grown from seeds in flats and nurtured to transplant size. Then the boxes were hoisted to the ledges, filled with soil and plants.

This same idea can be adapted for a house window. The box can be supported by poles, with the supports hidden by shrubs. You can also decorate a balcony with a box of this type and with lots of potted plants.

Before attempting this project, check with the building proprietor and with local regulations.

Snapdragons *grow tall in redwood planter box, decorated with carvings of giant replicas of Fusarium fungus spores.*

Late-blooming *chrysanthemum varieties, planted to replace fading summer annuals, provide winter window color.*

Zinnias, *dwarf dahlias, and sweet alyssum receive needed drink of water to keep up their colorful show.*

Bank *of marigolds, marguerites, juniper, gazanias, gerberas makes colorful surroundings for informal sitting area. Design: George O'Mara.*

Inviting entryway *has long, broad steps dotted with container plants. Large olive tree arches over ground cover of blooming yellow and orange gazanias. Clumps growing out of ground cover at right are agapanthus.*

Planning for Beauty and Function

Your reasons for landscaping are twofold—you want to create a garden that is usable and that is pleasing to the eye. This principle applies not only to the back area but also to the front and side yards.

First you must decide how you want to use your garden—just what are your family's needs. If you have small children, your landscaping scheme may tend toward a generous play area. If you want to entertain extensively out-of-doors, then plan for paved areas and for an easy flow of traffic from house to garden as well as through the garden. Perhaps you want a quiet place where you can sit and admire your garden. Then create a pocket in your plantings for quiet repose.

Once you have decided how to handle your functional needs, turn to the aesthetics. What kind of feeling do you want your garden to convey? Will the view of the garden from the house be pleasing? Will your garden be inviting? Plan your landscaping so that the garden is interesting not only to look at but to be in.

On the following pages are some solutions to particular landscaping needs. These designs are intended to give ideas and inspirations so that you can create a garden that you can live in and enjoy.

Redwood rounds serve as stepping stones, lead to pool in dry but woodsy area. Pool is man-made but looks like natural stream because of its secluded location, placement of various-sized rocks, and native ferns.

Japanese garden juniper, Juniperus prucumbens, *grows in and casually over hollow driftwood log.*

A Place for Plants and People

This garden serves two purposes. It is a place to grow and display a wide variety of plants (some rare, some common), paying special attention to their shaping or staging. It is also a cool, pleasant place for entertaining and relaxing. And it performs both these functions admirably on a lot 70 feet wide.

To accommodate a large and varied collection of plants, many container plants are used, and much shaping and pruning are done. Plants that threaten to elbow out some choicer neighbor are discarded.

One unifying factor is the use of neutral gray paving blocks throughout the garden. Another is the pervasive Oriental feeling, which results from emphasizing forms and textures of stone and leaf rather than flower color. Bright flowers are welcome for decoration, but the garden is essentially a green one.

Design: S. A. Sanfilippo.

Trio of Japanese pagoda trees shades and shadows terrace. Display pads under trees, benches hold flowers, bonsai.

Pinon pine (Pinus edulis), *planted in wooden collar, twists upward softening vertical planes of divider screen.*

A Garden of Continual Good Looks

Designed for year-round beauty, this garden has an all-green theme. The lawn is a thick carpet of dichondra backed by star jasmine, junipers, raphiolepis, and *Dodonaea viscosa*. Bordering the sidewalk are agapanthus and more raphiolepis. Blossoms of white burst in spring and summer when the star jasmine blooms and the tall stems of the agapanthus sport large flowers. Several evergreen pear trees pick up the structural feeling of the junipers and cast interesting shadows on the plantings and deck.

The all-green plantings and the reddish hues of the raphiolepis and *Dodonaea viscosa* complement the redwood of the house and deck. The deck, at house level off a screened-in room, provides a generous outdoor living area, including built-in perimeter seating. The deck steps down to a ground-level patio, an additional outdoor sitting area. The exposed aggregate patio turns a corner and becomes an angular walkway which leads to the driveway.

Landscape architect: Mary Gordon.

Garden *was designed for low maintenance. Lawn is dichondra, which springs back up after light foot traffic.*

Curving walk *connects driveway, patio. Beyond agapanthus at left is lawn; to right of raphiolepis is deck.*

View *of plantings from deck—evergreen pear in foreground, dichondra lawn, star jasmine, junipers, and raphiolepis.*

Redwood deck, *at house level, looks out on garden and patio. Perimeter built-in seating doubles as safety rail.*

Groves of trees *make house invisible from street, give it privacy and quiet of forest glade. Sunny, open but wind-protected lawn surrounded by pines on earth mounds seems as remote as a mountain meadow.*

Simple but Effective Landscaping

When this house was built, the only tree on the lot was a single, small native madrona. However, the owners wanted a secluded woodsy sanctuary. First the ground on the window side of the house was lowered and leveled, and the earth was shaped into several large mounds. Then pine trees 3 feet tall were planted in groves for immediate privacy and for wind protection.

The house sits on a knoll with the ground sloping off. These slopes were contoured to make them look as natural as possible. Then trees and shrubs were planted in groves, not in beds. Emphasis was on material native to the area: alpine firs, dogwoods, manzanita, Oregon grape, pines, sumac, and vine maples. There are also azaleas, bamboo, hemlocks, mugho pine, oaks, rhododendrons, *Viburnum davidii*, and yucca.

The only lawn is directly behind the house surrounded by pines. Silvery gray thyme creeping over the rest of the ground is pleasantly fragrant when you walk across it.

Landscape architect: William G. Teufel.

Driveway *winding up toward house is bordered by groves of different kinds of shrubs, trees. Emphasis is on natives.*

Country Landscaping

This house in the country presented landscaping opportunities that seldom exist on a city lot. It has no close neighbors. A rural road passes within 50 feet of the house; on the south and west sides, the house opens to look out on a 4-acre meadow, which slopes to a natural woodland of Oregon maples, madronas, and alders. The carport screens from public view a big, tree-shaded deck that opens off the kitchen and dining room on the east side of the house.

The landscape divides naturally into two main parts: the driveway-entrance on the north side, and a private garden world that spreads to the west and south.

The garden view from the house (see photograph below) includes the meadow and ends at the trees, the sweep of the meadow having been kept clear and unbroken. Only two wing-like plantings of low evergreens, 1 to 4 feet tall, embrace it, beginning on either side of the house and narrowing as they meet the woods. From the deck, a lawn of thyme flows down to meet a grass lawn that in turn spills into the meadow. Groves of trees at the foot of the meadow balance the bulk of the house.

On the north side (see photograph top right), the driveway and entrance plantings are designed for easy maintenance and to reflect the weathered silver of the shingled house with its charcoal black trim. Instead of grass, the lawn is another big patch of silver-gray thyme.

Evergreen St. Johnswort is the ground cover under the big linden tree east of the house (where the deck is). St. Johnswort is rugged enough to withstand summer drought and shade, and its good-looking foliage can absorb the tree's autumn fall of leaves, eliminating the need to rake. Between the St. Johnswort and the thyme are more than 50 low-growing rhododendrons which turn the slope to rose pink when in bloom in spring.

Landscape designer: George Schenk.

Entrance *has thyme lawn; across drive in foreground is Veronica officinalis between Photinia glabra shrubs.*

Sweet woodruff *frames drip troughs under eaves which are filled with crushed hard coal, repeating charcoal house trim.*

Sweep of *silver thyme flows down slope below deck to foreground where it merges with lawn and meadow. Two varieties of heather are massed at left of thyme; low rhododendrons grow at right. Deck is shaded by mature tree.*

Deck and Garden in the Woods

Once an overgrown clearing, this garden now includes a large raised bed, two redwood planters, a pathway of log rounds, and a deck that lets the owners enjoy their surrounding woods.

The deck, which extends the length of the house and around one side to the front door, has a flooring of 2 by 6-inch redwood, spaced ⅜ inch apart so needles from the forest trees can be swept through easily.

Alongside the deck, two planters were built to hold annuals for winter and summer color. The planters are made of 2 by 12-inch redwood and filled with rich topsoil from the surrounding woods; ¼-inch holes drilled in the bottoms provide drainage.

Around the deck is a path of redwood rounds and redwood bark to keep the natural look of the garden. The rounds were set into a wet, leveled bed of sand and cement.

Design: Tedd Wallace.

One of two *redwood planters built alongside deck holds cinerarias, a cymbidium orchid; box is 8 feet long.*

Redwood deck, rounds *look comfortable in woodsy setting. Rounds form path around deck, are embedded in mixture of sand and concrete; redwood bark fills spaces between. Planter in foreground holds fibrous begonias, coleus.*

Putting a Side Yard to Good Use

A long, very narrow side yard might be considered dead space by many homeowners. But this 50-foot strip was put to use and now contains a slim deck-garden. A 24-foot-long deck was built with a long, skinny garden and child's play area alongside it. Surrounding both the deck and garden-play area is a 5-foot fence, with space left for an edging of flowers.

The deck is made of 2 by 6-inch and 2 by 4-inch cedar; ½ by 2-inch cedar forms the wrap-around fence. Both are covered with a sealer to preserve the wood.

A flower bed, containing excavated dirt from beneath the deck, borders the deck on two sides. Growing in the bed are white alyssum, multicolored dahlias, dwarf yellow and orange marigolds, and single dark blue and white 'Magic' petunias. All the beds are mulched with bark dust.

In pots by the deck stairs, red-orange geraniums add more color. A Japanese maple planted in a sunken cedar box grows up through an opening in the deck. Lavender, red, and white fuchsias hang along the house side of the deck in cedar containers.

The play area includes a 30-inch-square sandbox with an overlapping lid that matches the deck and keeps out cats and dogs. Near the sandbox are small pines in containers and arrangements of river-washed rocks.

Also in this area is a long, 18-inch-high raised bed filled with bright flowers: sweet alyssum, yellow gloriosa daisies, multicolored pansies, white petunias, and red-hot pokers.

Design: Jacque Bowman.

Narrow side yard *is now a secluded deck, has enough room for relaxing, border plantings, and container plants.*

Lid *that matches deck fits snugly over sandbox, protects it from cats and dogs, disguises it when not in use.*

Sandbox *is part of play area. Nearby are petunias, small pines in containers, arrangements of river-washed rocks.*

A Garden Wonderland

Although this garden grows in a moist, benign climate, many of the imaginative features used in it could be employed anywhere.

The land came with big cedar and hemlock trees and the basic watercourse of the creek. But the ground was covered with a thicket of alder trees and salmonberry, and five running springs flowed from the base of one slope. Water from the springs plus the creek overflow flooded the flat parts of the property much of the time. Getting rid of the undergrowth was a simple but arduous matter of sawing and digging.

Converting the flatland beside the creek bed into well-drained terrain was the biggest task. First the rich topsoil was dug up and put aside. Then the creek bed was dredged to make it deeper, and sand and gravel from the dredging was used to raise the garden's grade. The topsoil was then spread over the sand and gravel in the garden beds, and at the same time many trees and shrubs were planted.

Next, tile lines went in to take the water from the five springs to the creek. So that the tile lines could also take away surface water, they were covered with gravel, and the gravel was covered with walkways of used brick.

The rich soil drains well enough now that you can walk and garden on it. But there is still enough subsurface water that the garden needs no watering. (You can duplicate this feature with an automatic built-in watering system.)

Design: Doug Verbonus.

Petal bench *around cedar needs an occasional inside trim to allow tree to expand. Pipe frame is set in concrete.*

Hollow cedar logs *(left) were filled with soil, then planted with sedum, saxifrage, sempervivum. Bridge (right) covering trout-filled stream is made of split cedar logs. Licorice fern, cottage pinks, pulmonaria grow at left.*

Sun filtering *through grove of cedar and hemlock trees warms entertaining area. Irish moss, lingonberry, cottage pinks border stream in foreground. Split log bridge provides passage from one side of stream to other.*

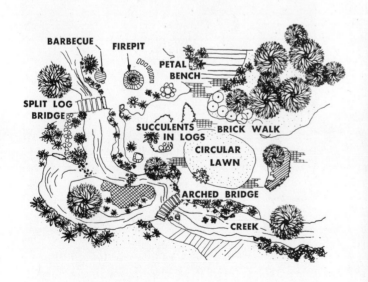

BARBECUE   FIREPIT

PETAL BENCH

SPLIT LOG BRIDGE

SUCCULENTS IN LOGS   BRICK WALK

CIRCULAR LAWN

ARCHED BRIDGE

CREEK

Narrow bridge *arches over calm section of stream where water lilies float; Japanese iris thrive at water's edge.*

A Flower-Vegetable Garden

This woodsy, heavily planted garden covers a hillside lot that once was half-covered with bulldozer scars, with an overgrown swampy area covering much of the rest.

To restore this land to a semiwild state, all the desirable native plants were dug up and set aside, then the brush and weeds were cleared away. The natives went back in the ground along with seeds, cuttings, and bedding plants.

The owners decided to develop several areas for vegetables, and they were interplanted with a variety of flowers and shrubs.

Much of the soil was compacted and had to be loosened with organic material, including compost, grass clippings, and sawdust. The weedy, swampy area had fairly good soil and needed less attention. A little stream was deepened to carry away water in some of the swampy areas.

Design: Richard Grimlund.

Plank cedar bridge *with protective railing spans creek. Bank in background flourishes with ferns, iris, rhubarb.*

Sunflowers *and strawberries decorate children's play area. String beans (out of picture) twine up swing supports.*

Vegetables *and flowers share a quiet corner. Compatible companions are beans, lettuce, and a climbing rose bush.*

Ravine Becomes Gardener's Delight

Once a blackberry-infested ravine, this garden now displays a wealth of plant materials. Hybrid rhododendrons make a background for low azaleas and dwarf rhododendrons. A bank of *Raphiolepis umbellata* merges into a grove of pines. *Magnolia denudata* and a Japanese flowering cherry 'Shirotae' are reflected in the pool.

Other plantings—corkscrew willow tree, junipers, a trio of blue spruce, Oregon grape, pink dogwood at the curve of the path, Spanish and Warminster or moonlight brooms holding a steep bank, ferns and Japanese iris along the water lily pool's rim, and a bed of rose red valerian—make this a garden for all-season viewing.

At the bottom of the ravine is a 30-foot-wide shallow water lily pool. The house sits on the crest of a slope 20 feet above the lily pond. A 3-foot-wide path, between the house and pool, is built of sharp crushed rock for stability and good drainage.

Landscape architect: Frederick E. Nylin.

White, fragrant *flower clusters of* Choisya ternata (*Mexican orange*) *show above their lustrous, yellow-green leaves.*

Wealth of plant material *is brilliantly displayed on steep banks of ravine. Steps of crushed rock climb from the shallow mirror-like pool to house. Garden was designed for year-round viewing from house and deck.*

Free-flowing Easy Garden

Although perched high on a hilltop, this garden has ample level space for outdoor living, play, and gardening. Graceful curves are the dominating feature—with a sweep of lawn bordered on one side by plantings and on the other by a patio. The exposed aggregate patio, shaded and shadowed by an overhead, is spacious enough for furniture and container plants which add splashes of color.

The patio narrows into a walkway which leads to a children's play yard and around to the front of the house. Flooring under swing set is contained between header boards.

Landscape architect: Mary Gordon.

Raised, covered *storage area for bicycles and play things is just beyond children's section of the back yard.*

Every place *in garden affords sweeping view of countryside. Design gives hillside lot ample level outdoor space.*

Border plantings—*star jasmine, raphiolepis, agapanthus, oleanders—complement curve of exposed aggregate patio. House was designed so every room has view through glass doors which provide easy indoor-outdoor access.*

Paving and rolling mound *of dichondra planted with trio of alders flow around weathered field stones. Walk has exposed aggregate finish, is laid in square blocks. In background, a roofed fence and storage shed enclose garden.*

A Nothing-Much-To-It Garden

The beauty of this garden is its simplicity. Several huge rocks, a cluster of alders, and a rolling mound of dichondra are all there is to it. You can stretch out on the dichondra or lean up against the alders; and you can't stop looking at those boulders.

The boulder in the photograph on the right weighs about 2½ tons. Garden supply yards often have rocks this size and smaller, called field stones, in stock. They sell generally for 2 to 6 cents a pound, and the price includes delivery on orders of more than a ton. You don't necessarily need rocks as large as the ones placed in this garden.

It's tempting to leave all of the stones sitting up on the surface of the garden for the full impact of their massiveness. But some here were treated like icebergs, buried as much as two-thirds underground. They look natural this way, not as though they had been dropped in as an afterthought.

The alders are extremely fast growers. Their root system is not a problem—occasionally a thick root reaches the surface, but this just adds to the naturalness of the garden.

Landscape designer: Mark Askew.

One sits up, *one lies down. Massive boulders appear natural, look as if they were always here. They weren't.*

Flowering cherry trees, *showing off their April blossoms, arch out over low-growing shrubs, are pruned in open and outward fashion to frame spectacular view. Long bench in background is for enjoying scenery.*

Huge bouquets *of white chrysanthemums decorate corners of 8-inch-deep pool. All jets are at work in the fountain.*

An Elegant Garden for Show

This garden is planned, planted, and maintained as a background for changing color. The most dramatic development occurs in the Z-shaped bed, which has a permanent edging of dwarf boxwood. Inside, for a brilliant summer-long display of color, it is planted with annual nemesia and Thumbelina zinnias. Then, when frost fades the nemesias and zinnias in the fall, they are removed and the bed is planted with daffodil bulbs for a spectacular spring show.

A bronze fountain from Italy provided the impetus for building the 8-inch-deep pool. The fountain and the pool occupy the central section of what was once all flower bed. Three valves control the jets in the pool and fountain. Various combinations of the value settings can produce a single jet from the dolphin's mouth, two series of five jets each along the length of the pool, and a pattern of five jets at the foot of the fountain. An electric pump recirculates the water at 580 gallons an hour. Jets can shoot as high as 14 feet.

A column of exposed aggregate supports the fountain figure. The pool itself is built of exposed aggregate concrete, darkened to give the water an appearance of depth. A brick cap tops the 10-inch-high curb.

Beyond the fountain, a steep bank falls away at the edge of the garden. A long, low bench placed there allows a splendid view of the skyline and also acts as a safety device for keeping people away from the bank. Two nearby flowering cherry trees have been pruned into horizontal patterns to permit an unobstructed view from the house.

Below the deck and along the wall of the house, a 20-inch-wide shelf holds pots of annuals in summer and narcissus in winter. The colorful displays can be enjoyed from both inside and out.

Landscape architect: W. David Poot.

Containers of petunias rest on shelf, give colorful summer show from inside house as well as outside. Winter-blooming plants replace petunias after they begin to fade. 'Thor' rhododendrons grow compactly below the shelf.

Z-shaped planting bed lines garden path, has dwarf box-wood frame. Summertime finds it full of zinnias, nemesia.

Same bed as at left is aglow with 'King Alfred' daffodils in spring. Planting area is in full view from the house.

A Formal Garden of Boxwood

A single species of shrub—English boxwood (*Buxus sempervirens*)—gives this garden much of its structure and decoration. This neat, small-leaved evergreen can be clipped or left to grow freely until it becomes a full graceful shrub or even a small tree. It is a slow grower (1 to 2 inches a year) and does not shed or litter. Where summers are hot, it should be grown in partial shade.

In this garden, topiary, the art of trimming plants into formal shapes, is practiced. True dwarf boxwood, *B.s.* 'Suffruticosa,' is trimmed to reveal sections of trunk between the three balls of green leaves. These 5-foot trees are 25 years old. They grow permanently in pots 3½ feet tall and receive an annual trim after new growth develops in late spring.

True dwarf boxwood, trimmed into globes about a foot high, edge the walk to the garden. Shrubs of bigleaf boxwood, *B.s.* 'Rotundifolia,' make up the thick green walls of the garden on three sides. The rounded, concave leaves of this lusty variety have a blue-green cast.

The garden is paved with concrete and decking. Plants used for touches of color are petunias, impatiens, daisies, and hydrangeas.

Landscape architect: W. David Poot.

Bigleaf *boxwood, 5 feet tall and planted 2½ feet apart in 6-foot-long boxes, makes effective patio privacy screen.*

Ball-shaped *boxwood makes low edging; clipped shrubs are about 12 inches tall. Topiary boxwood is in background.*

Topiary trees *of dwarf boxwood flanking walk in garden grow well in pots, so slowly they need only a yearly trim.*

Two-level deck *is screened for privacy from the street. Vertical 2 by 2's also block wind, create warm sun trap. Lower deck adjoins lathhouse at left. Space was left between fence and deck for border plantings.*

A Split-Level Outdoor Room

Two decks adjoining a lathhouse make a pleasant outdoor room. A screen of vertical 2 by 2's, lightened with occasional panels of cream-white translucent plastic, provides privacy from the street.

Each of the two decks—one 12 inches above the other—is only a few inches above ground. The gray stain used for both decks closely matches the color of the adjoining concrete carport floor and the round stream gravel in the lathhouse. The trellis above the decks follows the change of levels. The wood screens block the wind and create a warm sun trap, thus lengthening the deck's season of usefulness.

Shrubs, trees, and perennials were selected more for leaf texture and color than for flowers. The dark evergreen leaves of *Sarcococca ruscifolia* combine well with *Euonymus fortunei,* a glossy trailing evergreen. As a ground cover under rhododendrons, *Pachysandra japonica* repeats its whorled-leaf clusters on a smaller scale. And tiny-leafed *Pernettya mucronata,* when kept trimmed low, is an attractive carpet under tall deciduous azaleas. Closely clipped heathers group effectively near vine maples.

Landscape architect: Chaffee-Zumwalt & Associates.

Cool shade *of lathhouse suits hanging baskets—some contain fuchsias, ivy geraniums. Gravel floor absorbs water.*

Dividing Space between Generations

A projecting family room wing divides this rear lot into two separate sections—allowing a children's area on one side and an adults' area on the other. The house wing functions as a sound buffer.

The children's section has lawn, a play court, and built-in seating. The adults have a two-level outdoor entertaining room—the upper part is decking, the lower tile. Also included are built-in seating, a gas-fired barbecue, and a firepit.

Landscape architects: Hamilton-DiLallo Associates.

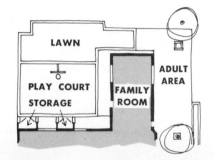

Children's section *includes built-in seating, lawn area, and lighted play court for basketball, badminton, skating.*

Adult and family *entertaining area, separated from children's area by projecting room of house, has built-in seating, raised firepit, gas-fired barbecue. Lower section has tile floor, upper level is decking.*

Activities in roomy sandbox can be supervised easily and unobtrusively from the deck above (left), which was designed for family activities (right) and adult entertaining. Deck is an extension of a paved patio.

Sandbox Below, Deck Above

Separating the play area for small fry from the activity area of their older brothers and sisters makes leisure more pleasant for the children and easier on the parents. This landscaping plan separates the areas and still allows for some parent or teen-age supervision of the young set and their sandbox play.

The main adult and teen-age outdoor play and entertaining area is a deck built off the house as a wood-surfaced extension of the concrete patio floor. It's covered at one end with a trellis (not shown in photograph) and edged around three of its sides with a long, built-in bench. Steps join this area to the lower part of the garden where the sandbox is.

Landscape architect: Lawrence R. Moss.

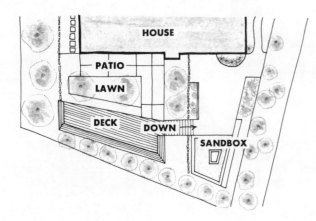

Toys are kept underneath wide rim of sandbox, so children don't track sand into house when gathering equipment.

Before: *Small house was enclosed by garden nestled into wooded canyon setting. Front yard was slightly altered when house was enlarged.*

Oak-shaded terrace *off dining room got new trellis, stone wall. New door from kitchen facilitates outdoor serving. Tree ferns set character of terrace. Plants include aeonium, philodendron,* Fatsia japonica, *camellia.*

Remodeling the Garden

There are several reasons for redoing a garden. You have purchased a home which has a garden that does not suit you. You have lived with your present garden for several years and want a change of pace outdoors. Your garden has matured to the point that it is too cramped and too shady—you want the outdoor space to be more open and useful. You no longer have the time to devote to the garden, so you want an easy-care situation. Or your family's needs have changed.

Before you remodel the garden, consider the structure of the house; the house and the garden should always work together. Replacing a porch with a spacious deck or decking over part of a lawn will affect the house as well as the garden. If your remodeling job involves structural changes to existing buildings, have all foundations checked. Also check with your local building inspector to see if you need a permit and if your plans need to be approved.

When remodeling an overgrown garden, first prune existing shrubs and trees to get a feeling of the basic framework. Capitalize on existing growth, then cut, discard, transplant, and plant. Use good-sized planting materials next to established ones. If you want a low-maintenance garden, avoid borders to trim and clip, annual beds to cultivate and change, and individual specimens to shape and care for. Contain lawn and plant beds with header boards, use ground covers and pavings, and build raised beds. If you lack outdoor living space and have more garden than you want, replace lawn and plants with a deck or patio.

Older section *of house is beyond added-on trellis-covered entryway. Remodel didn't destroy garden's lushness. Note trees, plantings that remained at left and right. Design: John Pitman.*

Revamping the Mature Garden

This 8-year-old garden was beginning to show some typical signs of its age. Shrubs planted close together for fast effect now competed for space. Shapeless plants hid parts of the house and blocked traffic on a walk that was too narrow to begin with. There were no sunny places for flowers. To improve the three main problem areas, the owners did some pruning, pulling out, transplanting, planting, and building.

The 4 by 6-foot planting bed to the right of the front door was overgrown with a narrow juniper and a bushy bronze loquat. The loquat had the most potential —big bold leaves and a strong trunk system—so the juniper was dug out. The loquat was heavily pruned to show its structure and its handsome, gnarly trunks.

To open up the entry, the old, undersized concrete walk and porch were replaced with a wood deck to make the entrance more inviting and to provide a place for container plants to be displayed. A Japanese black pine was planted in the deck area to the left of the front door in a 17-inch-wide flue tile sunk a few inches into the ground.

To the right of the garage, a blue Pfitzer juniper had grown to three or four times the size its owners had expected. As it had three sturdy trunks, it was pruned into a tree shape. Some of the full-sized nandinas next to the juniper were transplanted next to the loquat, some were discarded. Dwarf nandinas were placed under the pruned juniper.

Landscape architect: L. K. Smith.

Overgrown bushes *give crowded and closed-in feeling. Juniper (top) needs thinning and shaping; nandina will be dug out. Tall, pointy juniper (bottom) is being removed before loquat is pruned to show its handsome structure.*

Mature garden *needs some tailoring. Overgrown shrubs hide garage, cramp entryway, are crowded in small beds. Porch is too small and the walk is too narrow. Owners, consultant discuss ways to handle these problem areas.*

Decking *is 2 by 12's; 4 by 4 across front hides frame, edges bed at right. Pine grows in cutout at upper left.*

After pruning, *loquat shows handsome branch pattern, gnarly trunks. White vinca, nandina to right replaced juniper.*

Entrance *is roomier with juniper and loquat pruned and overgrown garden beds thinned out. You step up from driveway to new deck which provides open and attractive route to front door.*

A Complete Garden Change of Pace

This garden was remodeled so that it could be lived in as well as looked at. Located on a corner, the middle-aged house had an unobstructed view of the street from every room. The new design called for access and views to a series of gardens shut off from the street by fences and hedges. As a result, the living space is automatically extended to the lot lines.

Although the separate gardens that comprise the landscape differ in character from one another, all are meant to be walked through and lived in, as well as enjoyed from inside the house. Independent of each other, they are related by sight, sound, and repetition of plant material. Even the trees and shrubs in the woodland garden echo those used elsewhere.

The woods, fern garden, and trillium patch-service yard are fully planted gardens of mounds and hillocks with paths between them. In contrast, the gravel garden, spacious deck, and entrance are open spaces. In addition to displaying plant material to advantage, they work like rooms.

Landscape designer: Richard W. Painter.

Before: *Traditional wood-frame house was completely open to street; foundation plantings were simply shrubs, lawn.*

New entrance *gives house streetside privacy, easy in-out access. To emphasize entryway, gewgaws decorate roofline, and broad steps rise from sidewalk. You cross open garden pad to the front door.*

Formal garden, *hidden from street by hedge, has paths and bridges between planting beds and reflecting pools.*

Garden art—*fountain, carved panel, stained glass—decorates pebble terrace located between house and garden room.*

Close plantings, *dense foliage give deck woodsy feeling. A 6½-foot-tall screen maintains streetside privacy.*

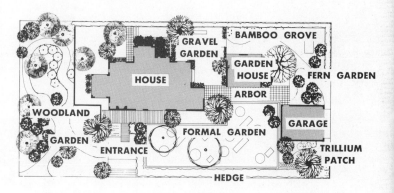

GRAVEL GARDEN

BAMBOO GROVE

GARDEN HOUSE

FERN GARDEN

HOUSE

ARBOR

WOODLAND

GARAGE

GARDEN

FORMAL GARDEN

TRILLIUM PATCH

ENTRANCE

HEDGE

Old House Gets Fresh Start

Adding a deck and privacy screen across the front improved the looks and the living qualities of this older L-shaped subdivision house.

The basic aims were to create privacy, to add usable outdoor living space in front, and to improve the lines of the house. The new 10 by 22-foot deck is at floor level of the house. The living room now opens through a sliding glass door to a garden-like area, bright and visually exciting as the sun plays on a translucent glass screen.

Bricks set in sand in the running bond pattern form a walkway between the driveway at the side of the house and the deck. Papyrus (*Cyperus papyrus*) and Japanese aralia (*Fatsia japonica*) grow tall through a ground covering of ivy. The feathery papyrus create interesting shadows on the screen.

Design: Don Sharpe.

Sun creates dramatic patterns on translucent glass screen. Sliding glass door separates house from new front deck.

Before: *L-shaped subdivision house had simple lines, lacked streetside privacy and usable outdoor living space.*

New front *follows plane of projecting wing at left. Beam across front and line of deck emphasize horizontal. Glass screens keep the entry deck private. Protected from wind but open to sun, outdoor room is warm sitting area.*

Floor-Level Deck Replaces Porch

This 50-year-old house was situated on a fairly large lot (60 by 104 feet) and was hidden from the street by a 60-foot-wide strip of trees and plants. However, the garden as well as the house needed remodeling for aesthetic as well as functional reasons.

The entry was moved to one end of the house, and a bridge was added for easy access to the front door. The living room was opened out through large glass windows and a pair of doors (where the entry originally was) to a new floor-level deck and a view into the thickly planted park strip. A slat screen separates the entry from the deck.

The roof line did not change on the house, but the covered porch was removed.

Design: The Bumgardner Partnership.

Before: Entry was simply a small porch; front door opened right into living room. There was no outdoor living space.

Bridge leads to new entrance placed at one side of house. To left of freestanding slat screen is deck addition.

Deck, garden are extensions of living room. Glass windows, screen doors provide good inside-outside transition. Behind camera, entry path winds up through thickly wooded area to street and parking area.

Before: House, patio, and garden lacked transition. Also, patio was too small; grassy slope was largely unusable.

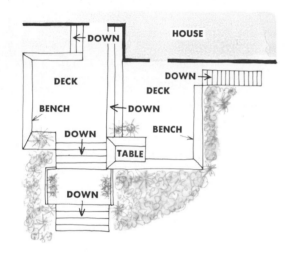

Decks, steps *were built over existing grade. You walk out at floor level, have choice of two decks or lower garden.*

From House to Decks to Garden

Enjoying a garden as an outdoor living area usually depends on how accessible it is from the house. If you can walk into it at floor level, it becomes an extension of the house.

Before the deck and step addition, this house was almost a classic example of separation of house and garden. The main living area, raised 3 feet above a two-level garden, was reached by concrete steps that were functional but awkward. The concrete sitting area was located on the uppermost garden level, and access to the flatter lower level was along a grassy slope, not the most desirable pathway after a rain.

Outdoor furniture was hauled out for summer use, but there were no permanent seating surfaces, such as built-in benches.

That situation was changed by a new system of decks and steps that take you out of the house at floor level, then entice you down into the lower portion of the garden by generous steps broken by a deck-sized landing. Benches are built in on both decks, and there's an additional bench beside a gravel path that leads from the foot of the steps to a paved play court.

The upper deck is 15 by 20 feet, the lower one, 15 feet square. Both are surfaced with 2 by 6's. Step treads and benches are 2 by 3's on edge spaced ⅛ inch apart. Decks and steps are edged with 2 by 4's, benches with 2 by 6's.

Landscape architects: Jongejan-Gerrard-Associates.

U-shaped *built-in bench provides permanent seating, allows space for table. Railing defines end of top deck.*

Deck, Terrace for Outdoor Living

Before remodeling, five narrow steps separated the kitchen from a garden area that had no real usable outdoor space. When the kitchen was redone, a glassed-in breakfast area and a small deck were included to overlook the terrace. Large oblong concrete stones set in gravel (used as a ground cover) provide firm footing for outdoor furniture on the terrace. Wood rounds serve as stepping stones and direct you around the garden.

Design: Kaye Scott.

Before: *Kitchen door opened to flight of steps leading to garden, which was generally left in a natural state.*

Native oak *branches over gravel terrace. Deck at floor level of house makes for easy access from inside to out.*

Small deck *off breakfast room is supported by posts resting on granite blocks. Concrete stones, wood rounds, gravel surfacing look right at home with native oaks. Container plants can be brought to deck for color.*

Garden of Good-Looking Surprises

This front landscaping job involved building, enclosing, and partially roofing a small patio and shade garden at the front of the house. The purpose of this remodel was to block out the sight and sound of a busy boulevard and to make the front yard useful. The design also created an unusual welcoming entry at the driveway and front-door end of the area.

Design: Ernest L. Nickels.

Front of house before (top) was plain, had no usable outdoor area. Remodel (bottom) gave house outdoor living space (through a brick-enclosed patio), and a secluded and pleasant entry.

Platforms of 2 by 4's form entry bridge, act as stage for potted plants. Chrysanthemums add splashes of color.

View is from carport, looking over entry bridge into private patio. Pots at right hold oxalis, shamrock, jade plant.

Plants *at entryway are rosemary,* Pinus roxburghii, *hanging ivy at left; chrysanthemums, Japanese black pine at right.*

Secluded patio *(viewed from house) has built-in bench, overhead, potted plants, brick floor, decorative objects.*

Railroad ties, *4 by 4's make raised bed. Jade plant cuttings are rooting in bonsai bowl; santolina is at left.*

River-smoothed *stones and bunches of creeping, fragrant rosemary make harmonious ground cover companions.*

Deck Solves Garden Dilemma

Having more than enough garden to maintain yet no usable space for outdoor living is a fairly common problem. This garden was heavily shaded, so the lawn was usually damp. The lawn was too sloping to be useful, yet many hours were required for its upkeep.

The solution was a large two-level deck, supported by concrete pillars, easily reached from the house, and placed to get as much sun as possible; a paved game court; and a garden designed for minimum maintenance.

The result is a garden but no lawn; the grass was replaced with gravel, paving, and decking. Shrubs and flowers are in raised beds. The game court can be used for a wide range of activities—basketball, badminton, paddle tennis, tetherball, skating, bicycle riding.

Design: Glen Hunt & Associates.

Before: *Shaded lawn was wet underfoot during rainy weather; slope had limited use. Existing deck was small.*

Path *goes from carport around deck to play court and garden. Plants are bamboo, azaleas,* Daphne odora, *ferns.*

Two new decks, *oriented to catch maximum sun and take advantage of view, are at living-room level of the house.*

Game court *and deck cover most of former lawn area. Rectangular concrete pads in gravel carry foot traffic to court.*

Deck Creates Outdoor Living Room

Before the addition of the deck, this lot had a good-sized lawn but no real place to relax and entertain out-of-doors. The 12-foot-wide deck is an extension of the family room—it can be reached from that room or from a balcony (also added in the remodel) leading to the front door. Because the lot slopes, the open end of the deck is supported by three posts.

Overhead rafters provide interesting shadow patterns on the deck and slightly filter the sun. The section of the deck facing the street is screened with evenly-spaced boards which give privacy to the deck but still allow light to seep through.

Under the deck is a carport—corrugated aluminum suspended under deck joists directs rain runoff and keeps the car dry.

Design: Glen Hunt & Associates.

Before: *House lacked usable outdoor space and transition from inside to out, had blocky feeling.*

Deck addition *forms roof for carport, adds large, convenient outdoor room, improves exterior appearance of house. Screens give front section of deck privacy from street. Beam across front unifies new and old.*

PHOTOGRAPHERS